Trapped

Copyright © Keith Hearn 2025

ISBN- 9798323878734

Book cover photograph copyright © Keith Hearn 2025

By

Keith Hearn

Trapped

The book is dedicated to my lovely mum, it is a story of the last years of her life. Including her battle against the terrible disease Vascular Dementia and Alzheimer's.

I hope my story will help others to spot the early signs of a loved one who might be going through the early signs of Dementia or Alzheimer's.

Margaret May Hearn

1935 – 2024

Mother, grandmother and great-grandmother

Trapped

Contents

Chapter 1	*Smoke Screen*	*1*
Chapter 2	*The Journey*	*37*
Chapter 3	*Shocking News*	*63*
Chapter 4	*Mum's Demise*	*73*
Chapter 5	*The Inevitable*	*95*
Chapter 6	*The Fighter*	*120*
Chapter 7	*The Writing On The Wall*	*162*
Chapter 8	*Realisation*	*183*
Chapter 9	*Goodbye*	*201*

Trapped

Acknowledgements

My family, brothers, their families, my daughter, son and grandchildren.

During the time of writing the book. My mum became seriously ill with Vascular Dementia along with Alzheimer's. Sadly in February 2024 mum passed away.

To all the NHS staff who during my mum's illness helped me to care for her.

Dr Read at Gratton Surgery, for being there whenever mum's health took a turn for the worse, and everyone at the surgery. And of course all the District Nurses.

Beccy from the Countess of Brecknock Hospice, Andover

Everyone from Winchester Hospice, who cared for mum during her last days.

To everyone living in my village and the Running Horse pub who showed such kindness.

Thank you

Trapped

No Regrets

At Times Life is very hard.

Never Give Up

Life is far too short.

Give life your best shot and make a go of it.

Never look back and never give up on your dreams

The rewards for hard work are immense.

Dreams can come true.

Keith

Trapped

INTRODUCTION

The book is about my late mothers journey as she negotiated the effects of Vascular Dementia and Alzheimer's.

The title of the book reflects her demise and how as her full time carer I also became trapped in the cycle of her diseases. It takes nothing away from my mum's horrendous demise.

Within a relative short period she went from an independent, determined and incredible person to a shell of her former self.

Both Dementia and Alzheimer's are cruel diseases, to watch a loved one fade away in front of one's eyes is devastating, for everyone.

I would never wish the curse of dementia and anyone.

Trapped

Chapter 1 – Smoke Screen

This story has been hard to write because it is a story of my mum's journey and her sad decline in her health more so, having been diagnosed with both Vascular Dementia and Alzheimer's. I hope this story will serve to help others who might be going through a similar journey with a loved one. During mum's journey, there were many things that at the time were hidden from view as to what was happening to her and at times were also hidden from me. Initially, I had no idea what was happening to her. I shall try to explain a little more about my mum's background, as children my brothers and I were used to her being a very determined, feisty, and somewhat bloody-minded person. Whenever anyone in authority, i.e. Doctors or Nurses, asked if she was feeling alright her normal answer would always be "oh yes I am fine, I could not be better, I do not know what all the fuss is about", these phrases will be quoted many times throughout the book. As a child mum's family were dirt poor and more so when her father Rodmond sadly passed away at an early age and quickly she had to learn to survive and to stick up for herself.

The story regarding her dementia journey began a few years ago, it must have been around 2019 just before the first lockdown in 2020. For me, it began with a telephone call from mum's doctor and at the time mum was living alone in her bungalow located in a village just outside of Swindon, Highworth. Her doctor explained to me how mum had fallen over just outside of her bungalow where she was then taken to the local surgery to be patched up, it was found she had a nasty cut just above one of her eyes and a few abrasions above the other. Apparently during a walk from the bungalow to the local shops, she had to climb a bit of a slope to get to the shops it was

Trapped

along the same footpath where she had been found on the ground and was unable to get herself up and back onto her feet, along with the cuts above her eyes she was also badly bruised around her face. I was at work at the time and informed her GP I would take the following day off and we agreed to book an appointment for both mum and I to speak to the doctor. Later the same evening I spoke to mum on the phone, of course, she said "look Keith I do not know what all of the fuss is about, there is no need to take time off from work as I am OK, please leave me alone". I explained to her how I was extremely worried about her recent fall and having been found on the ground injured in the street, I confirmed with mum I would see her first thing the following morning.

At the time I would contact mum every morning to check up on her and to make sure she was OK, I would check on her ever since my dad passed away in 2004, a long time before the current spate of falling over. I would visit her every second weekend, and we would go shopping mainly for food. The first thing I would do whenever I entered the rear door of her bungalow was to check her fridge/freezer and the cupboards within the kitchen, the majority of the time there was little food inside the fridge freezer. Every fortnight I would bring her staples such as tea bags and biscuits, some of the things were items she liked but would not buy only because she thought some things were far too expensive. On my trips, we would visit a garden centre and she would buy a bag of compost along with some plants, she enjoyed her trips and would look forward to me taking her to the shops. It was soon time for her doctor's appointment, and I managed to get the following day off work, the college where I worked was very good whenever it came to letting me have time off, to visit my mum. Early the next day I arrived at her bungalow and mum opened the rear door, and immediately I could see the nasty-looking bruising around both eyes, it was mainly around the brow of her eyes I think it was the right eye where she had a dressing placed along the brow. The first thing she said was, "don't fuss or have a go at me", I assured her I was only concerned about her falling over and subsequently hurting herself, she just brushed my concerns away. We entered the living room to sit down and had a nice cup of tea, where I then tried my very best to explain to her about having booked an appointment with her GP for later the same morning and at the time I was surprised only because she did not argue with me, she was adamant I came with her, I explained it was why I had come to see her and yes I would be with her when she saw her GP. She seemed to be a little more relaxed, I truly believe she knew deep down there was a possibility something more serious was happening to her health-wise, but mum being mum, she would never open up or let anyone know exactly what was worrying her.

So, it was we eventually walked up the same hill to where only the day before she had been found collapsed on the pavement. At her appointment, mum was called forward to see the doctor. After about half an hour, her GP walked into the waiting room and called out my name, she wanted me to come with her to join her inside the consultation room where by now mum was sitting in a chair, I could tell by the look on her face, something was wrong. Mum was agitated and she virtually shouted "I am not a nutter and you are not going to put me in a nut house, do you hear me", I explained to mum no one was going to put her away in a mental institution or anywhere else, the GP tried her very best to reassure mum no one was going to put her in any institution. There was something far more serious going on and it was possibly why mum kept falling over. The GP went on to explain she had examined mum's eyes, and she found she had cataracts. Also, her eyes were a milky colour and she would require a cataract operation, in the doctor's opinion mum would need operations on both eyes. The doctor was going to refer mum to an

Trapped

eye consultant at the Great Western Hospital in the meantime I would need to book an eye test with a local optician, who would be able to confirm how bad the condition was and after an inspection and checkup of her eyes by an optician they would inform the eye team at the Great Western Hospital, GWH Swindon. But it wasn't the only thing her doctor had found; she carried out a basic cognitive assessment on mum and sadly she failed the test. This was possibly the reason why she had said she wasn't a nutter. The GP informed me she would be informing the Memory clinic of her initial findings and confirmed with mum there would be a follow-up appointment with the hospital. Mum asked me if I would be by her side when going to the hospital. I replied, "of course mum, please remember you are not on your own" she replied, "thank you". We then left the surgery to walk home, and beforehand mum wanted to go to a shop in the village when she entered the shop many of the local people asked her if she was feeling OK. She didn't really reply to their questions instead, she made a joke and said, "this is my toyboy", indicating she was talking about me, then said, "I am only joking, this is my son Keith". Introductions over with she went to pay for a few items, the man behind the till knew who I was and he told me it hadn't been the first time mum had been found in the street and had fallen over, I was by now well aware of the fact mum had fallen over more than once, my stomach was doing summersaults. It was at this point I felt I needed to somehow move her away and out of the bungalow and into my house. But it was easier said than done.

As we walked down the hill and home, there were so many things running through my mind, everything her GP told me had hit me like a sledgehammer. It had made sense to me regarding her eyesight, at the same time I must admit I wasn't too worried about mum failing the cognitive test, as I was more concerned about her eyesight because I thought it might be the reason for her falling over and with

Trapped

hindsight deep down there was a much more serious reason. As we entered the bungalow I knew there and then, if she did not have the operations to fix her cataracts her life would become far worse for her and would also lose her independence and she would not be able to live on her own, if she eventually became blind if she did not have such a simple operation. The significance of her having failed the cognitive test did not register with me and as such I did not fully realise the significance of the test. My concerns at the time were about mum falling over at the time I thought it was because she could not see properly and as such the priority was to try and persuade her to have cataract operations to correct her eyesight. As we sat around the dining room table drinking a cup of tea, mum said to me "I don't know what all the fuss is about, I am OK, and I don't need any operation". I got up from the table and contacted the local opticians and explained the situation regarding what mum's doctor had said and an appointment was booked for the following week and as I was talking to the receptionist, I could hear mum say in the background "I am not going to get my eyes seen to, as there is nothing wrong with my eyesight just get off the phone and please stop telling tales". After booking mums appointment I sat with her and I tried my very best to explain what the doctor had recently told her, at the same time, I knew full well the magnitude of what was said to her, it hadn't sunk in, with mum, as I often mention she was stubborn. I tried my very best to gently explain to her the damage that was being done to her eyes and she urgently needed the cataract operations if not she would eventually go blind, and there would be a point of no return if no action was taken and would be far too late to correct the damage. Mum's initial and somewhat predictable reaction was to hysterically refuse any operation on her eyes, she went on to tell me her eyesight was perfect and there was nothing wrong with her eyes. It was a typical reaction and one everyone within the family would not be surprised.

Trapped

The time soon came for mums optician appointment, at the time I could tell she was nervous and of course, she was very worried, which was understandable and as we entered the optician where a lady then called her forward and took mum into an examination room, once the optician had finished what she had to do, she came into the waiting room and asked me if I could enter the examination room, and I found mum was sat in the examination chair. Before the optician could speak mum said, "It's alright Keith there is nothing wrong with my eyes, we are leaving now". The optician said, "Mr Hearn I am afraid as you are no doubt aware, your mother requires cataract surgery on both eyes, I don't know how your mum has been able to get around". I explained about the falls and she replied "I am not surprised I am afraid your mother urgently requires the operations sooner rather than later, I can see your mum has a milky film across both eyes, I shall send the results to the eye clinic at the Great Western Hospital and I will forward a copy to your mothers GP", she asked mum if she had any questions regarding her examination, mum blurted out "I just do not know what all the fuss is about, as there is nothing wrong with my eyes, Keith is overreacting as usual". The optician replied, "Your son Keith has done the right thing" With that mum, and I left the opticians we went for a nice cup of tea at the local tea shop. Inside the tea shop we had a nice cup of tea and of course some cake, after placing her cup of tea onto the table mum looked at me and she said "Oh Keith will you promise me you will be with me when I have my eyes operated on won't you?" I replied, "course I will" I held her hand it was at this point she knew it would be OK; she just needed some reassurance, it was well known within the family she would always fight against going anywhere near a hospital. She had a few weeks to wait for her appointment at the eye clinic at the GWH. Initially, it would be a consultation with a surgeon long before any eye operation. She was duly called forward for her first consultation, I took a day off work to be with her while

Trapped

she attended the consultation. This was going to be the start of a journey and neither one of us had any idea of how it would end. I think one of the major reasons why my mum had such a fear of hospitals was, in this case, because the Great Western Hospital, GWH, was where my dad had been admitted in 2004 alas, he never came home. As children, I and my brothers had a great childhood, like most families we had our ups and downs, what family doesn't? Before my dad sadly passed away mum was his full-time carer, before dad became terminally ill and once again, he made me promise to look after mum. It wasn't the first time dad had asked me to look after mum. The first time was back in the 1960s, I was around about 9 years of age, it was when as a family we were living in South Arabia, not to be mixed with Saudi Arabia, the country is now called Yemen, as a family we lived in the main port city of Aden. At the time dad was serving in the British Army and he served in an area called The RADFAN it was a border region the local terrorists were backed by Egypt and were fighting against British rule. In Aden we lived in a relatively peaceful area, which is not to say there weren't any terrorist attacks on the British Military and their families. Dad would visit Aden on his Rest and Recuperation, R&R. We only went to school in the mornings as it was due to the extreme heat after school, mum would drag all three of us boys, come what may, to the British military beach. One day at the beach dad told me whenever he wasn't around, I was to look after mum and of course, I had taken what he said to heart because dad had placed such a huge burden on my shoulders at such a young age. He may not have known what it meant to a child so young and of course impressionable I took everything he said to heart. My responsibilities carried on long after dad passed away, in a way I am glad dad had instilled in me a sense of responsibility because I looked after mum late into her life. Getting back to the story of mum's cataract operations.

Trapped

Things were never straightforward whenever it came to mum, nothing new there then? Mum was never the easiest of people to "organise", I am not sure if it is the right word to use, or to explain my mum's inner mind. At the same time, we were waiting for her cognitive test at the memory, GWH. Mum was still living on her own in her bungalow and I was living in Winchester, it was not an easy drive if things ever went wrong regarding mum. As mentioned, I would visit her every fortnight on a Sunday, but whenever her eyesight affected her, I would travel each weekend to make sure she was coping and to take her shopping, I was still contacting her by phone each morning. Since my dad sadly passed away in 2004, I would contact her daily to ensure she was OK and to check her post. I remember one particular Sunday I was sitting at the dining room table, and I began to open her post, I would always read each letter to her and explain what the contents meant. One of the envelopes had the NHS logo/stamp on the cover, I suspected it was her appointment for the eye clinic. Of course, it was a long-awaited appointment for her to attend the eye clinic and for mum to have a consultation with a surgeon who would carry out the cataract operations. The letter went on to explain the surgeon was going to operate on her left eye first, I think it was the worst of her eyes. I explained what would happen when she attended the appointment and all of a sudden she shouted "I am not going, because what happens if I cannot see anymore, I don't want anyone messing with my eyes", I was expecting such a kickback from mum, I truly believed by now she realised just how serious things were and of course, at the same time I understood she was somewhat scared of the unknown. I replied, "if you don't let the surgeon at least take a look at your eyes before your operation, you will no doubt go blind". Her response was as always, "will you be with me", my reply was "of course". She thought it over and said, "OK Keith I will go to the appointment, please promise me you will come with me"? Of course, I said yes. With that, we attended her

Trapped

consultation with the surgeon, as mentioned it would be the same surgeon who would be carrying out the cataract operations. The waiting room within the eye clinic was packed and it was a little bit like a conveyor belt of people, some people had already had their eye operations and were waiting for a post-operative check-up also there were people just like my mum who were there to have a pre-op consultation. It was mum's turn to see the surgeon, she was somewhat reluctant to see him only because at the time I was told to wait outside of the consultation room. I knew it would not be too long before I would be asked to join her inside the consultation room. A nurse informed me the surgeon needed to speak to me. In the consultant's room, mum was sitting on a chair along with various pieces of optical machinery situated close by, the surgeon went on to explain to me mum was refusing to have the cataract operation. I calmly talked to her about what would happen to her, if she did not have the cataract operation. I soon managed to get her to agree to have the operations the surgeon ten asked her various questions regarding her eyesight and one of the questions was along the following lines "Mrs Hearn how long has it been since you noticed you have problems with your eye sight", her reply was "I don't have a problem with my eye sight and I don't know what the problem is? My eyesight is perfect". He replied, "Mrs Hearn if I do not operate and very soon, you will eventually go blind so please listen to me and let me perform the cataract operations". He handed her a consent form allowing him to perform the cataract operations. She looked at me and said, "What do you think Keith"? I replied "mum please sign the form and just get it over with", When she tried to sign the consent form, I had to point out to her where the line she needed to sign she still managed to sign over the dotted line and the surgeon looked at me we both knew full well she could not see the line.

Trapped

The surgeon thanked me, and he pointed out mum's surgery appointment should come through in about a month's time.
We left the room where she almost ran out of the eye department and as we got into a lift to the ground floor of the hospital, she said to me "I hate these places, please get me out of here, let's go home and have a nice cup of tea, I am dying for a cup of tea, and added, "you would have thought they would have asked everyone who was waiting if they wanted a cup of tea, wouldn't you"? During the drive to her bungalow, she once again asked if I would be with her when she had the cataract operation and once again, I reassured her I would be with her.

At her bungalow, the post had arrived and once again there was a white envelope with the NHS logo on the outside of the envelope. By now she had made both of us a nice cup of tea. I asked her if she wanted to open the post, she asked me if I could open the post for her and read out whatever the envelopes contained, most of the post was junk mail apart from the envelope with the NHS logo. I duly opened the envelope, and I could immediately see it contained an appointment for mum this time it was informing mum to attend the memory clinic at the GWH. I read out the letter and her response were to say, "oh whatever next, why can't they leave me alone". I explained to her it was a different appointment. I went on to explain to her it was the follow-up from her doctor's recent memory test. I once again took a day off work to be with mum during her latest hospital appointment, her memory clinic appointment was before her cataract operations. It was soon the day of the appointment, and we arrived at the hospital early on arrival at the department the doors were locked, next to the entrance where there was a buzzer along with a security camera monitoring access. There was a sign on the door pointing out the department wasn't open for another thirty minutes. On the way to the memory clinic, I noticed a café, Mum and I visited the café for a cup of tea and coffee. I found somewhere to sit and asked her if she wanted something to drink "oh yes please, I am gasping for a cup of tea and could I please have a nice piece of cake" I thought to myself, that's unusual as mum very rarely ate in public, apart from the quaint tea shops. I purchased a cup of tea along with a cup of coffee and a chocolate muffin. Mum drank her cup of tea and of course she thoroughly enjoyed the muffin. Looking at mum it did not look as though she had any issues with her memory but at the same time, I knew something was happening to her and although at that precise moment in time, I was far more concerned regarding her loss of sight.

Eventually after a cup of tea and the muffin, we were able to access the memory clinic. I booked mum in at reception, and we sat in the waiting room for her to be called forward. It wasn't long before she was called forward and mum along with a nurse entered a side room after roughly five minutes I was asked to "pop" into the same room, and a nurse explained to me mum had refused to participate in the memory test, unless I was in attendance. The clinician who was going to test mum's memory went on to explain to me I could attend but I must not help mum during the memory test. During the test, I could see firsthand just how bad mum's memory was and I felt so sorry for her, a few times she looked at me for help during the test. As such I was not surprised when she was told she failed the memory test, I wasn't officially told she had failed, but it was so obvious to me she had. The clinician informed mum and me that the results of the test would be sent to mum's GP, and a consultant would examine the results, and they would recommend any further treatment, or if need be further tests.

At the same time, only a few weeks after the memory clinic appointment mum's first cataract operation appointment came

Trapped

through, and by now it was March 2019, needless to say, mum had successfully undergone eye surgery on her left eye. During her recuperation, she stayed with me in Winchester. Mum had previously stayed with me on many occasions ever since my dad had sadly passed away. She would often stay with me in the summer months and of course at Christmas. By now it was late spring, and she was to stay with me enabling me to administer eye drops three times a day and to change the gauze covering her left eye, she also had to wear a see-through plastic eyepiece to protect the left eye. During her recuperation from the surgery, I would take her for walks through the village to the local stud, she enjoyed this particular walk where we could look at the horses outside running around in the fresh air, trotting and running around the fields, including the many wild animals such as deer, rabbits and squirrels. It was such a happy time for her, and she loved being outside in the fresh air observing nature around her and of course the horses. I would take my camera to take lots of photographs of the animals, at the same time I would explain to mum about the deer and what breed they were. I would point out to her the robins who were drinking from the horse's water troughs in the fields, she always looked happy and relaxed during the walks, taking in the views along the fresh air. Mum was always at her happiest walking in the countryside watching the horses scamper in the fields alongside their newborn foals. She would tell me if she had the money, she would have purchased a farm and filled it with different animals. Mum's eyes would often light up with excitement and full of happiness. These were happy times and as such I could see she was at peace with the world. During her recuperation and on the walks she would at times look just like a pirate, what with the white gauze including the plastic eye patch covering her left eye. As always, she looked forward to getting out of the house and to be able to go outside, I believe the walks somewhat distracted mum from

Trapped

thinking about having cataract surgery, she was very easily distracted.

Mum was an outgoing person along with a wicked sense of humour, one which not everyone appreciated. On many an occasion whilst on our walks we would bump into people who I knew, and I would introduce them to mum. Obviously during the walks, she was still wearing an eye patch covering her left eye and it was a source of interest. Nearly every time she was asked what happened to her eye she would respond "Oh Keith hit me" and then laugh. I would hastily reply to inform the person who had enquired, and I would go on to explain how my mum had recently undergone cataract surgery. At the same time, she thought her comments were hilarious because in her mind her comments were very funny, but for others who were not as tuned into mum's sense of humour, her comments were seen as somewhat bizarre, to say the least. During the spring and summer months, the village looked wonderful bathed in colour with many flowers in full bloom along with the well-kept gardens, the hedge rows also the trees covered in blossom. So was as she was recuperating during her post-operation on her eye and by now it was coming up for seven weeks once again she had an appointment at the eye clinic at the Great Western Hospital for a checkup on the cataract operation, it was to be with the same surgeon who previously operated on her damaged cataract. We arrived at the hospital and before seeing the surgeon a nurse removed the eye dressing and cleaned the eye ready for the surgeon's consultation to then assess how successful the cataract operation had been. We had a bit of a wait then it was mum's turn to see the surgeon, once again she entered the consultation room on her own and once again the surgeon opened the door to his consulting room and asked for me to sit with mum. I sat listening to what he had to say and as he asked mum some questions, she did not seem to understand and he responded with "I do not know what you are saying, you can ask my son Keith if you want to"? I did my very best to answer some of the surgeon's questions, of course there were questions with which mum had to answer herself, after explaining the surgeon's questions he had asked her, she was by now able to answer. Eventually, the surgeon was satisfied his questions had been answered and on checking her left eye, went on to explain to me, and of course to mum he was happy with the results, he informed mum she now had 90% of sight restored in the left eye. He was somewhat flummoxed when she responded with "I can't tell any difference"? He examined her right eye as he was also going to be the surgeon who would carry out the second cataract operation. At the same time, he told her he could not foresee her having the operation to correct her eyesight until late 2020 or possibly early 2021. Mum was more than happy with the news only because she was averse to hospitals along with any type of operation. Of course, in her mind, if she could put off any stay in the hospital, she would be so happy. After the consultation she wanted me to take her back home to her bungalow, in the village of Highworth. Once again, I had to leave her on her own at the bungalow, of course, I was reluctant to leave her on her own, but at the time it was the situation in which we had found ourselves. Mum was determined to live on her own and to also keep hold of her independence, I have to say I would be the same if I ever found myself in a similar position. I would fight for my independence for as long as it was humanly possible. Summer 2019 came and went, as I have mentioned mum would stay with me during the summer holidays and as often as possible. She did her normal thing on her "summer holiday", which was to sunbathe, and I would always look after her hand and foot, I did not mind as she deserved a nice break to help leave her troubles behind. At the time she was still able to climb the stairs to access the second largest bedroom, she would often refer to the bedroom as her "B&B room" oh how she would laugh at her jokes. I would always

Trapped

decorate "her" room and keep it looking crisp sharp and fresh for her stay. Whilst I am writing about my mum's bedroom and my thoughts drift back to Christmas not long after my dad had sadly passed away. Mum was once again staying with me over the Christmas and New Year period. Every Christmas I would prepare the Christmas dinner just as dad had done. He and I would cook the turkey and various meats on the 24th of December a day before Christmas day. This particular 24th December it was early morning I had only just placed the turkey into the oven. When all of a sudden, I heard a crash coming from the direction of mum's bedroom. I rushed upstairs and knocked on the door of her bedroom. I heard a muffled "Come in Keith, help me I am stuck", once inside the room I could see the bed had collapsed as I moved further inside the room, I could see mum was bent double and her bottom was resting on the floor. The headboard, to the bed, was intact and it was standing upright, and the mattress was at the bottom of the bed, and it was resting on the floor. Poor mum, luckily, she hadn't hurt herself and I could see she was in some discomfort. As I tried to get her out of bed she began to laugh and at the same time, I felt relieved to find she hadn't hurt herself. I should have taken a photo of the scene before me. I then helped her to get out of bed, she was able to walk downstairs to go to the toilet and get herself a bath and change into her clothes. Meanwhile, I visited the garden shed where I found some wood glue and long screws. I then managed to glue and screw the bed back together. I thought of the incident only because by now her health had declined and she was by now unable to climb the stairs or to dress herself or wash herself, how things had deteriorated since then.

Over the remainder of 2019, I would visit her at her home and began to see a slow decline with her mental health. Sometimes I could see she wasn't cleaning the bungalow to her previous high standards, for instance, her living room carpet was badly stained and from what I

Trapped

could tell the carpet had at some time had tea spilled on it. Once I saw the stains along with other things to do with the cleanliness of the bungalow, I would often bring along with me a more powerful hoover and a carpet cleaner. I would have to make up excuses whenever I brought along with cleaning equipment, as I did not wish to embarrass her or upset her in any way. It was during 2019, and mum's GP once again contacted me. This time it was because mum had been found close to the local shops, a passerby had found her collapsed on the ground and they could not get her back onto her feet, she was eventually helped to the local surgery where her GP assessed her and a nurse patched up mums various grazes. The GP asked me if I could visit her the following morning, which I did. Meanwhile, a nurse had kindly walked mum home, and she asked her neighbour Jenny if she could keep an eye on her until I came to see mum. First thing the following morning I drove from Winchester to her village and I knocked on mum's kitchen door, I hadn't told her I was visiting and sat her down and we had a cup of tea I explained about my visit to her GP, and the reason why. Mum wasn't happy, as she did not know what all the fuss was about, she went on to say, "I only slipped over, and everyone is making such a fuss". I duly went to see her GP and she informed me it was well known in the village my mum was falling over whenever she left her bungalow to visit either the surgery, Chemist, or the local shop. Her GP was somewhat concerned about mum's situation, also without the official results of her memory test or an assessment of her mental health, be it Dementia or Alzheimer's as there was very little the GP could do. I informed the doctor I would be taking mum home with me because things by now were progressively getting worse. As I walked down the hill towards mum's bungalow, I was determined to bring her home with me and to live with me to keep her safe and sound, I knew I had to be tactful to get mum to agree to come home with me. She was on the council's home line service, and I contacted them, and I informed them mum

Trapped

was coming back with me to stay in Winchester, on a short "holiday". Of course, she was sitting listening to what I was saying and of course, she overheard what I had said and said "you didn't tell me I am going on a holiday to yours, I haven't packed anything" we both knew it would not take too long for her to pack some clothes and for her stay at my house. I can still remember as she enquired about what her doctor said to me at the time I thought mum knew something was happening to her, but she did not want to discuss the matter, and I left things at that. She always felt safe with me besides by now it was November 2019 as mentioned I always brought mum to my house to have Christmas and New Year with me, I helped her pack some bags and placed them into the boot of my car before we left her bungalow I helped her with the post which had by now mounted up. We had a quiet journey to my house at the same time I knew something was on her mind, whenever I asked her if everything was OK, she would respond "Never mind me just keep your eyes on the road". Needless to say we arrived at my house and as we entered the village we passed the local pub and she would always say without fail "that's where all drunks go" She would then laugh and my response was always the same "hey cheeky I drink in there" she would respond "exactly". She was a very cheeky monkey with a very sharp tongue. By now she was ensconced at my place for Christmas 2019 and the upcoming New Year 2020. During the morning of New Year's Eve, I had a phone call from the eye clinic at The Great Western Hospital. A nurse informed me someone had cancelled their cataract operation and so the surgeon wanted to operate on my mum's right eye, but it would have to be the same day, I jumped at the chance, and I agreed for mum to have the operation. After the phone call, I informed mum of the operation on her right eye and of course, she became agitated at the same time she was very worried and of course it was understandable. I went on to say to her, it was an opportunity for her to finally have full sight restored in both eyes

Trapped

it would be very worthwhile to have the operation on New Year's Eve as it would be a great start to 2020. She saw sense and knew it would be over with later the same day. We eventually turned up at the eye clinic early afternoon and we waited for mum to be called forward for the operation on her right eye. Whenever we waited for any medical appointment, we always talked to allay any fears mum had and of course, it was a very nervous and tense time for her. She would tell me, "if it wasn't for you Keith and I was on my own I wouldn't have all these medical procedures or the operations" I would always respond "I know" also everyone within the family knew full well what mum, gran and great gran was like. It was soon mum's turn to be called forward for her operation by now as it was approaching 5 pm and the darkness had descended on a winter afternoon. I wished her luck, and she handed me her handbag, informing me her purse was inside, and she knew exactly how much money was inside. That was mum all over. After an hour or so I was called into a side room where mum was sat with a gauze and a plastic shield covering her right eye. The nurse went through the treatment and explained to me that someone had to apply eye drops to mum's eye, it was the same medication I had recently applied to her left eye. I was so pleased she had opted for the operation and at such short notice, I knew it was the best thing mum had agreed to do. To be honest, I do not think I could have coped with caring for a blind parent, more so my mum, only because as mentioned she was such a live wire and full of life. It may sound unkind, but she was somewhat of a difficult person when she had all of her faculties long before being diagnosed with dementia and more than likely going blind.

If she had become blind, life would have been so difficult for both of us. As we headed into 2020 thankfully with mum's eyesight restored. After eight weeks she was to attend an outpatient appointment once again at the eye clinic she had her eye cleaned and for the surgeon to

Trapped

check on her eyesight and discharge her from the hospital. The surgeon was happy with the results of her surgery, and he was more than happy to discharge her from the clinic. Mum was still living at my house in Winchester, and we drove to her bungalow to pick up any post and for her to have a chat with her neighbour's and to also to pick up her prescription from the local chemist. On the way back as we drove to Winchester and we stopped off at Tesco's Marlborough where we purchased the food she liked to eat, by now it was getting late in the day and we still had a bit of a drive to Winchester, even though it was New Years eve the traffic on the roads was fairly light. We arrived at my house and mum all of a sudden and from out of the blue she began to argue with me and she demanded to be taken home in the morning, by now I was very tired and asked her if we could talk about her returning to her bungalow in the morning. We then ate an Indian meal, and you would never have known mum just had a full-scale argument. Peace had at last descended on the house.

At the same time January 2020, there were various stories on the national news regarding a virus emanating from out of China. At the time there weren't any serious warnings, it was a story rumbling along with other mundane world news. At the same time no one was very alarmed at what was happening within China. Sometimes the news could be somewhat misleading, and it was not accurate, because China at the time was releasing what their government thought the World authorities should know regarding the virus. No one knew anything about the devastation which was by now heading our way. After mums all clear regarding her cataract operations, I decided to take her home to her bungalow because by now she had been couped up at my house for far too long, and she was climbing up the walls, at times she was just like a caged animal who needed to run outside to be free as a bird and to be able to do whatever she wanted. Mum went home sometime in early March 2020 at this stage the British

Trapped

Governmental scientists were releasing press statements regarding the virus spreading from within China by now it was a worldwide pandemic. There was one thing I could never understand, and it was why the Government hadn't restricted or stopped flights landing in the UK. The news was becoming concerning also at this point there was talk of a "lockdown". Regarding mum, there was something niggling at the back of my mind. One Saturday morning in March I phoned her, and I spoke to her regarding my fears, and I asked her if she wanted another break at my house, she agreed but only if I could take her shopping in Winchester and of course I agreed. So it was one Sunday morning I drove to her bungalow and the first thing she did when I walked into the living room was to have a cup of tea. Mum cooked breakfast for me and the thing about my mum was whenever she cooked, she would either cook food until it was black and charred and inedible, or it was virtually raw and there was never any in between. Subsequently, I had a plate of meat placed in front of me of course, the food looked raw and I asked her to pack her bags and while I ate the breakfast she went into her bedroom I quickly scraped the plate of raw meat into a bin bag and then took the bag to her general waste bin outside. Just as mum was struggling through the living room with her bags of clothes and she looked at the table and said, "My you must have been very hungry Keith". With that I took the bags from her and placed them into the boot of the car. I then "booked" her out with home line and left to return to Winchester via Marlborough and of course Tesco's supermarket.

After mum's successful cataract operations and was eventually cleared by the surgeon it was at this point, I knew her eyesight had thankfully been saved and of course, I was relieved and very happy for mum.

Trapped

It was by now approaching the end of February 2020 and the news emanating from out of China along with the media and British Government by now the news was sounding ominous and was somewhat alarming. At the same time no one knew what was coming our way nor of the implications for the whole world. For a certain mother and son living within a small rural village outside of the ancient city of Winchester, there were far more serious matters on their minds, matters which affected them directly.
It would not be very long before events within the wider world would directly affect everyone living within the village and for that matter all villages, towns, and Cities across the country for that matter across the whole world, meanwhile there was a surreal sense of quiet before the oncoming storm. At the time mum and I were living in our little bubble, my mum was by now adjusting for the first time in a long while and she was enjoying the luxury of being able to walk, unaided without the fear of falling over and being able to walk to the nearby countryside. We were both geared up to take mum home to her bungalow in Highworth, Swindon, we agreed I would take her home at the end of March 2020. My garden looked colourful along with the daffodils in bloom and the tulips looking resplendent in their many bright colours.

Each morning mum and I would watch the news on the TV, and we knew things around the world were becoming worse by the tones of the scientists and the government ministers. One particular evening the Prime Minister was on television to address the country. It was at this point he announced the country was to be placed on a "lockdown" as of the 23rd of March 2020. At the time no one could guess what was going to happen of course, no one at the time knew how the world would change and would not recover for many years, nor how many people in the country and of course the world would sadly die all because of a deadly virus. At the time the world news

Trapped

was reporting thousands of deaths within China, I could not understand why the British Government had not stopped all flights from landing within the UK's airports whilst the COVID-19 virus was creeping across the world having seemingly originated in China itself. At the same time, the Chinese government denied the virus had originated within the country. Eventually, all flights into and out of China suddenly stopped by now it had taken what seemed like an enormous, long time for flights to eventually be grounded.

At the time China was a titan of global exports and still is, during COVID-19 worldwide trade suddenly came to a juddering halt by now nothing could leave China, it was all due to the COVID-19 virus which by now was spreading across the world.

Early March 2020 Mum and I were tiny cogs within a worldwide disaster by now was heading our way, I think we both thought things could not be so bad at the same time we had some faith in the government. When the first lockdown was announced, the country was in a state of shock, I took the view if the government were recommending a national lockdown and of course it was for everyone's safety the government wanted to protect the people of the United Kingdom. If only we truly knew what was going on behind the scenes of government, more so No 10 Downing Street. At the same time, there were more and more announcements on both TV and Radio regarding the effects of the COVID-19 outbreak. There were announcements regarding hospitals around the country which were buckling under the strain of the COVID-19 outbreak. Mum and I were lucky enough to be able to go for our walks into the countryside and they would have to stop, it was hard to explain to mum why she could no longer go outside and at the time she could not understand what harm a walk into the countryside could do to anyone. Very soon it was impossible to go to the shops to purchase food. It was during this time I started to use the internet to purchase food deliveries online. Whenever the delivery drivers turned up they were fully masked up and wearing gloves and whenever a delivery driver turned up at the house to drop off the delivery I would be masked up having made some room for the driver to drop off the food and kept a safe distance from one another the atmosphere at the time was alien to everyone. This was a minor inconvenience compared to what was by now happening across the world, also the UK hospitals and care homes. At the same time Mum and I continued to get on with our lives within our tiny family bubble, as best we could. Mum did not fully understand what was going on, she still wanted to go outside and to be able to go for a walk outside and to be in the wonderful fresh air. As I keep repeating everyone within the family knew mum, gran, and great-gran who enjoyed the fresh air and going for long walks and of course she was always happy to be outside enjoying nature, my main task at this time was to keep her entertained and to keep her busy, of course during lockdown it became even harder to keep her "entertained". Luckily spring was by now unfolding and of course, the warmer weather was heading our way also on top of the fresh air and the long walks mum was a sun goddess and her skin was mahogany brown due to her love of sunbathing. It was somewhat of an obsession with her.

It soon sunk in with mum she would no longer be able to travel to her home, to her beloved bungalow. It was at this point when the arguments began I did try my level best to live a stress-free life, by now it was impossible to travel anywhere, due to the lockdown and by now normal travel was non-existent and it was out of the question to drive mum home. Of course, it was all my fault and at the time it was a small price to pay. Time and time again I had to explain to her what a national lockdown meant but of course, it never sunk in. It was at this point during early 2020 I began to think there was indeed something wrong with mum's memory and sadly at the time I put it down to old age, I know it may sound patronising. The longer the lockdown went on, the more arguments occurred and as such I would have to plan what I could do to keep mum active.

My mum had always been a feisty and argumentative character, and she would never take fools gladly. Within the family, she was well known for being extremely stubborn. During the years of looking after and caring for my mum, I soon realised what my dad had to put up with during their married life, I have to say he must have had the patience of a saint. I do not think I could have put up with her, but of course, they loved each other, and she was also my lovely mum. The irony was towards the end of her life living suffering from both vascular dementia and Alzheimer's and now she could no longer remember much of her early life some days she did not even know who I was, by this time the feisty lady had all but disappeared she would never return, it was so sad to watch my mum slowly disintegrate in front of my eyes.

It was by now full lockdown across the country, and it is sometimes known as lockdown one, the daily news regarding COVID-19 was by now the main news topic. Such words as pandemic were thrown around like confetti at a wedding, figures were being used on graphs, by scientists and politicians to emphasise how serious the situation was becoming, I would look at the graphs along with the figures at the time I could not grasp the many thousands of people who were dying on hospital wards or at home. It was at this stage I got to hear on social media that someone I had previously served with in the Army had sadly succumbed to the virus and sadly passed away from catching COVID-19, it was sad news. I thought of my mum, and I thought to myself, we had been very lucky so far, especially with mum being the age she was at the time.

During May – June 2020 the lockdown rules were slightly relaxed it meant up to six people could meet outside or within a park when

Trapped

outside everyone had to social distance for a distance of up to two meters. As we watched the news and the announcement regarding leaving the house mum only had to hear the words "allowed outside" suddenly she responded to the news, "right Keith I am going to pack my bags and you can take me home"? it took a long time to calm her and to try and explain exactly what was meant by the announcement and she truly believed I was deliberately keeping her at my house under duress, it was the farthest from the truth. Even though the country was by now in a lockdown situation, people were still allowed to go for a walk but only in family groups within their own "bubble". So it was both me and mum who would once again be able to walk to the local stud and visit the horses by now as it was fast approaching the end of March 2020. In places, there was a frost on the ground, before going outside I would have to make sure she was well wrapped up for the cold weather and at times I was concerned about her because she hadn't a clue as to what to wear, whenever she went out for a walk in the cold weather. Once again, I ignored the signs that something was very wrong with her. At this stage in 2020, mum was more than able to walk more than 3 miles unaided she was a strong walker. Whenever we returned home the first thing, she would ask for was a nice hot cup of tea along with a countryside cake. Soon after her cup of tea and the cake she would have a little snooze on the couch. At the time I had no idea the walks would be one of the last occasions she would be able to manage to walk to the Stud, it was very sad. During one of our walks to the stud and as we returned home, we observed lots of people surrounding one of the horse bays, David the stud manager asked if I could refrain from taking photographs of the horse and stable. It was then I suddenly twigged, and it was because a horse was about to give birth to a foal. My mum did not have a clue as to what was unfolding before our very eyes. As we walked home, I explained to her what was about to happen within the stables and she replied, "oh that is nice". We

Trapped

walked home to have a nice cup of tea and some tasty cake. A year or so later I would reflect on those happy days taking mum out for a nice walk into the countryside, at the time we took the simple thing such as going for a walk for granted. Now I would give my right arm to take my beloved mum on a long walk into the local countryside. I will never take my freedom to do what I want to do for granted.

Summer of 2020 my front garden was a bit of a mess it was the perfect time to tidy it up a bit and clear out the weeds, it would not be a quick job, and so it was, I soon put mum to work as my garden labourer, of course, she jumped at the task. The front garden was a bit of a "dead zone" as nothing much grew all because of eight leylandii trees which at the time were growing in my next-door garden, my neighbour David had previously approached the council time and time again to have the trees removed. All of the trees were covered in thick ivy mum, and I initially tackled the ivy along with the many brambles growing on my side of the garden. Mum truly enjoyed herself and, of course, she enjoyed helping me work outside once again she was able to be outside in the fresh air. After tidying the front, we bagged over thirty bags of garden waste. At the time all I had to do was wind mum up like a clockwork toy and she would have quite easily worked through the night, which is if I did not drag her indoors. She was such a hard worker and always enjoyed helping me, we had so many laughs and at the same time we made so many fond memories. With so many trees growing in front of the house the front lacked sunshine during the summer months and was even worse during the winter months.

Towards the end of July and the beginning of August 2020, the first lockdown enforcement slowly began to be relaxed, of course, mum soon caught onto the fact the lockdown rules were to be eased and new rules were to come into force and at the time I wasn't so sure. Every morning mum would start the morning off with an argument as she was adamant she wanted to go home to her bungalow in

Trapped

Swindon. After a week or two I relented and reluctantly took her home to her beloved bungalow. I warned her if there was to be another lockdown on the horizon, I would not hesitate to bring her back to my house. I reluctantly took her home to Swindon of course, she was so happy and at the same time I kept warning her I would return. The easing of the lockdown rules did not last for very long and during October 2020 I returned because the government had called for what I termed as a "mini" lockdown. I have to say she didn't seem at all surprised and strangely she seemed somewhat relieved, during the journey to Winchester she began to tell me about "pigmies" who were attacking the front door of her bungalow and she said they were living in the bushes in front of her house. She went on to tell me about the many telephone calls during the night and went on to tell me of "a lady staying at the bungalow and how the council had given the bungalow to her". I was concerned about what she told me. I have to say at the time I was more worried about the lockdown along with the COVID virus. On the 5th of November 2020, the government announced a second lockdown. By December 2020 the second lockdown was relaxed and mum's surgery contacted me to book her in for the first mass rollout of the COVID-19 vaccine. Before Christmas, I drove mum to Swindon the Steam Railway Museum where a mass vaccination program was to take place for the elderly and for those who had certain medical conditions. We queued for hours after a long time we were eventually at the front of the queue where a doctor read out a list of medical conditions and why someone could not have the vaccination, one of the medical conditions on the list was an anaphylactic shock? At first, mum said "I had bee stings, it was when my Ron was alive", Ron was my late father. I remembered the incident I informed the doctor the bee sting had happened over thirty years ago, he replied: "I am afraid your mum cannot have the vaccination even though she was stung thirty-odd years ago, it is because the vaccination could bring on another

Trapped

anaphylactic shock". Mum was beside herself, I once again calmed her and said, "Mum they cannot take the risk please let's go home and have a nice cup of tea". Before we set off, I needed to get her to a toilet only because she would not be able to make it home, often I would have to plan journeys around toilet facilities. We then quickly left the museum and of course we were very disappointed alas we could not do anything about the situation, even the medical staff did not know at this point how the virus was going to pan out or how many people would eventually die. I knew one thing it was I would have to keep a very tight rein on mum until there was a vaccination and one which would not affect anyone who was susceptible to anaphylactic shocks. Until then I needed to have eyes in the back of my head to ensure she would not be put in a position where she could catch the dreaded virus, it was far easier said than done. As mentioned, because she was a live wire and was someone who did not like being told what to do, that was mum all over. I have to say at this point I think she did understand what was happening around her, such as when we had to queue for the COVID vaccination along with lots of other people all waiting to have their first jab at the railway museum in Swindon. Whenever something new was raised on the news by a scientist or a politician and at the time they were trying to explain to the nation when there was a change in the pattern of the virus or the statistics regarding the ongoing deaths. I would try my very level best to explain to her and in words she would understand. Even though she could not understand why the nation had been placed into lockdown, she did not like being told where and what she and the rest of us could do, such as having to remain at home inside our family "bubbles" she was slowly getting used to having to isolate of course it did not mean she liked it. At the same time, her eyesight was much improved and she wasn't falling over anymore and was much steadier on her feet, even so, there were small things she would say to me, and at the time I could not put a finger on what it was.

Trapped

There was a positive side to the situation, at least my brothers and the family knew mum would be safe staying with me and it allowed everyone to get on with their own lives. During this time, I did not realise just how much I was taking on, more so when eventually mum did not know what time of day it was. At the same time because of the virus and it was seemingly easy to catch, it was compulsory to wear face masks, luckily it was easy to buy masks along with lateral flow test kits online. On top of the national pandemic during 2019-2020 I was worried about mum's eyesight, and I was trying my hardest to ensure after the operations her eyes were being tended to. Making sure she had the eyedrops three times a day and changing the gauze covering her eyes. One of the more awkward things was to make sure she was not removing the plastic covering her eyes and to prevent dirt from getting into her eyes and of course, stopping mum from touching her eyes. I have to say it was not an easy task. Once she had been checked over by her consultant, he confirmed the operations had been successful. Once again she told me if it hadn't been for me being with her each step of the way, she would never have had the operations obviously if she had the operations and was on her own she would never have used the eyedrops once again that was mum all over. Hence why I was slightly sidetracked from mum's other issues, such as seeing pigmies along with a woman and her family who had taken over her bungalow. It is well-known mum who never asked for any help, and she would just brush off any ailments or illnesses and would instead bury her head in the sand, thinking her illnesses would disappear of their own accord. Then as soon as any ailments deteriorated it would be all hands to the pumps scrambling to get her medical help. We all seem to forget just how scary the oncoming worldwide pandemic was, and it was an unknown situation one the world had never seen in living history. On top of this, I was fully aware mum was by now a ticking time bomb waiting to go off. The outcome of mum's health would slowly

Trapped

become apparent it would take a long time to raise its ugly head. At the time I missed any if not all, possibly some of the alarm bells and I believe at the time I was distracted and did not know what to look out for. In between the two lockdowns when mum was able to live at her bungalow and as previously mentioned I would phone her each morning to check to see if she was OK, I would ask her if she was feeling ok and her reply was always " I am fine things could not be better" of course I could read between the lines and I am afraid I sometimes took what she said as a pinch of salt. I knew she would say what she thought, and I wanted to hear she only said it to get me off her back. Also, every Sunday, if it was permissible I would visit her to ensure she was well and of course to make sure she was buying food for herself. The first time I visited her after a lockdown her bungalow always looked nice and clean there again after a couple of visits I began to notice the odd stain on the living room carpet and marks on the kitchen worktops, it was unusual for mum, as she was house proud, at the time I did not say anything to her, as I did not want to embarrass her also I did not think it was fair to visit and to then begin to point out these things to her. After a few trips, the stains were still visible along with yet more stains. There was also a bit of a whiff, I knew immediately it was the strong smell of disinfectant. Poor mum, I soon realised she could not cope living on her own, I knew I would have to put a plan of action together to try and move her out of the bungalow and for her to live with me. During one of my Sunday visits I brought with me a hoover along with a carpet cleaner and a few cleaning sprays. When she saw me with the hoover along with the carpet cleaner she would take offence and I would quickly made an excuse by telling her it was the best time of year to have the carpets cleaned, once again I did not wish to embarrass or to make her feel inadequate. Mum was such a proud lady and it certainly was not my place to belittle her in any way, hence why I made up stories to make her feel better and to make it

Trapped

sound as though it was her who thought of the idea to clean the carpets, etc. At the time it was the small things I noticed within the bungalow, the place she enjoyed living in, it was not at all like my mum's. One of the things she enjoyed doing was attending to her precious front garden and on each visit, I would take her to a local garden centre, and she would always come home laden with compost and plants, she was always happy in her garden. I never forced mum to come to stay with me as she was always happy to stay with me. She called the bedroom where she slept at my house her "B&B Room" it is still the "B&B Room". I knew mum's bungalow was her last vestiture of independence and her "freedom" It was the freedom to live on her own and to do whatever she wanted. Alas overtime it would all be taken away from her.

There again it would take so much time along with a lot of persuasion on my part to get mum to see a doctor or to attend any medical appointments, she would often say "if I was on my own I would never see a doctor or attend any appointments", alas it was mum all over. As her son, it was frustrating for mum to have such an attitude regarding her health. At the time I was working part-time and the coordination of "sorting out" mum's administration along with her many appointments on top of all of this the COVID-19 pandemic. It was not easy to drop everything to try and sort mum's life for her. Saying that I never once had a problem with work or taking time off whenever it was needed. There again regarding mum nothing was easy and looking back on this period, I did not realise mum must have been suffering in silence, because no one at the time was aware of what was happening to her, and of course, she would never tell me how she was feeling. There again I did not have a clue as to what was happening bearing in mind at the time I was only visiting her once a week.

Trapped

The main issue was the fact I only visited her every Sunday at the same time mum would ask me to take her shopping to do things around the house for her. At times I did not have the time, I know it sounds like a poor excuse, to check on her health, I had taken her shopping and I would fix things around her bungalow and read the post for her, it would soon be time to travel home to Winchester, sometimes I wouldn't get home until the early evening, or later if there had been a traffic accident on the A34. On the odd occasion, I could not visit mum due to snow drifting in around her village and I would have to turn back home, at the time I would feel guilty. Then there was yet another occasion when I was driving the car I was traveling from mum's place the car developed a mechanical fault, the engine blew up. I still remember it as though it was yesterday. During one of my trips long before the COVID pandemic I was returning from visiting mum one Sunday I had just driven through Savenake forest outside of Marlborough whilst I was driving along a local A road I could see a car in front of me it was only traveling at @20 MPH I safely overtook the car and as I did so I could see the occupants were an elderly couple who were out on a Sunday afternoon drive, I got safely past their car then I heard a noise coming from under the bonnet of the car and the car suddenly lost all power, the old couple passed me on the inside whilst my car was by now traveling down the hill at one point we were traveling parallel and the couple had a look of surprise on their faces as my car traveled backward. Luckily there was a layby close by and I managed to steer the car safely into the layby, to cut a long story short the AA eventually came out the recovery driver informed me my car that my head gasket had blown and the pistons were seized and as such the car was very badly damaged and it was in his eyes a write off he towed me home and I sat in the passenger seat of the recovery vehicle. I got home later the same evening and phoned mum to let her know I had only just got back home with a badly damaged car.

Trapped

She panicked and the first thing she said was "are you still coming to see me next weekend?" I replied, "Of course I will. In the meantime, I purchased a cheaper car from a local garage.

Once again towards the end of 2019, there were rumblings regarding a second national lockdown and I decided before it became impossible to drive anywhere in the country, I made arrangements to travel to Swindon to bring mum to my house. Mum didn't seem surprised, obviously, she wasn't happy about the situation there again. She was used to staying with me over the years, so it wasn't too difficult to persuade her to come home with me. Besides she began to realise if there was indeed another lockdown, I would not be able to visit her on a Sunday. As we packed my car I managed to strap her into the passenger seat once again it was not an easy task with mum, she was too quiet for my liking and as I looked over to where she was sitting I could see she had managed to put the seatbelt around her neck and as such she could not attempt to pull the seat belt into its lock. I tried to pull some slack on the seat belt but was unable to do so on checking what the problem was I could see she had somehow managed to shut the passenger door onto the slack of the belt. After mum stopped fighting, I opened the passenger door and managed to secure the seatbelt. As the car pulled away she said to me "Oh are we going to collect my prescription" I then stopped the car to open the back door to her bungalow and she said "no I meant at the surgery" I drove to the surgery and of course they knew nothing about her prescription so I had to explain the situation luckily they fast-tracked the prescription and gave me the paperwork to walk to my mums chemist once again I explained the situation to a pharmacist and luckily they knew about mum it then took ten minutes to make up mums prescription. I got back to the car where mum said, "what took you so long" I looked at her and thought to myself "Keith don't explain just drive". We got to Marlborough where we as usual

stopped off at Tesco's, I managed to get mum to the toilets and after some shopping we then drove home. We were lucky only because at the end of October 2020 the government went on to announce there was to be a second lockdown, it would come into force in November 2020. I got mum safely to my house and just in the nick of time.
At the time mum's memory lapses were becoming more noticeable and she was repeating herself and becoming frustrated with herself, once again at first, I had ignored her symptoms, but after a while, the symptoms became much more frequent.

By the end of 2021 it was noticeable mum was becoming more unstable on her feet, but she wasn't falling over, not yet, but whenever she walked around the living room I noticed she needed to grab hold of the furniture to help stable herself and once again whenever I enquired if she was OK. I have to say you would have thought I had accused her of stealing because she would rip into me and would tell me to stop interfering in her life and to leave her alone also for some reason she added "don't fuss I am fine don't you dare tell any more tales to your brothers, I know what you are like". After a few hours over a cup of tea of course along with a piece of cake, she would apologise to me for her recent outburst. I tried my hardest to try to explain to her why I contacted my brothers, Michael and Garry, and it was because I needed some help and advice from them and to be able to share my concerns regarding mum. During the period of mum having problems with her eyesight, I kept my brothers updated with her diagnosis and of course with mum's operations. She often tried to put me in a very difficult position and of course I went against her wishes. There was some good to come out of the lockdown and the pandemic, if you could call it "some good" it was regarding food deliveries, during the lockdowns the deliveries were somewhat of a blessing in disguise. For me, it helped to ease the pressure more so my mother's declining health. The practice of ordering online has continued to this day. There are many things I would do before the pandemic and have changed for the better.

Early December 2021 the second lockdown rules were slowly being relaxed but not enough for me to take mum home to her bungalow besides it was only a few weeks before Christmas day. Once again mum and I were able to go outside on short walks to the Stud and the countryside. During the winter months, I would take my camera with me and would take many autumnal photographs of the countryside of course of mum and the horses. As we walked through the village towards the stud area and whenever we saw someone, we would walk on the opposite side to them or hop onto the verge to let them safely pass and to give as safe distance as possible, once again it was a strange world. The ability to be able to walk into the countryside was only a short distance from my house and was a godsend during both of the COVID-19 lockdowns. More so for myself, having to "entertain" mum for hours during the day only because she did not know why we were couped up inside the house for so long. I class myself as being extremely fortunate to live in the countryside during the time of the lockdowns as millions of others were not as fortunate. It enabled me and mum to get out into the fresh air and as mentioned mum was somewhat of a fresh air freak.

She was a feisty character and was somewhat of a free spirit and of course she did not care what she said to people she could be somewhat blunt. As mums' health declined it was very sad to see her feisty character decline, I was beginning to become more and more concerned about her state of mind. But alas at the time I was not fully aware of what was affecting her mental health, obviously I knew her memory wasn't as sharp as it used to be. I think I put it down to old age as she was by now 86 and of course, she would never tell me how she was thinking regarding her health. As it was

Trapped

becoming difficult to decipher her symptoms, I did not know where to start.

Chapter 2 – The Journey

During the second lockdown and towards the end of 2021 mum informed me she was running low on her prescription medication. She wanted me to drive to her village to submit her prescription. I once again informed her we could not travel anywhere due to the lockdown restrictions and for her not to worry as I could submit the prescription to my surgery, it took a few days it was eventually agreed mum could pick up the prescription from my surgery in Winchester, but there was a proviso at the time no one knew what the future would hold or how long the lockdown restrictions would last for, all due to the pandemic. The proviso was for mum to give permission for my surgery to transfer her medical records from her own surgery and my surgery and it would make things much easier. She would then have medical cover provided by my surgery. Everything was sorted and I felt so much happier as mum by now had medical cover provided by my surgery and of course they would dispense her medication. At least I would not have to travel from Winchester to Swindon every time she required a prescription. Frequently I would broach the subject of mum coming to stay with me for good and to live with me and on a more permanent basis. Her response would always be "oh no I would not like that, because we would never get on and besides I like my independence we would only fight". On the other hand she did not mind living with me, but only when she was on "holiday". The beginning of her "long stay" was during the first and second lockdown. It took many attempts to try to try to get her to understand I could not keep "jumping" in the car and then to drive her back to Swindon, whenever there was a slim chance of a lockdown rules being relaxed. During the first lockdown as I have previously mentioned we would watch the news, I did this to show mum it wasn't me "making up" the lockdowns or the rapid spread of the deadly virus. Of course she would always listen to what the then prime minister along with what the scientists had to say. Over a period of time the seriousness of what was happening it was by now slowly sinking in, I truly believe she began to understand it was not me, stopping her from going home. It was during the same period I noticed she was not lifting her feet whenever she walked around the house and it was more of a shuffle. Also she was having episodes of forgetfulness, once again I am afraid I put it down to "old age", I was more concerned about the shuffling motions and falling over and then seriously hurting herself.

I have mentioned it previously I could not talk or get through to mum, my many concerns regarding her health, as I have mentioned she was a very strong willed and such a stubborn person with a mind of her own, I felt whenever I tried to explain to her regarding my concerns and observations I was hoping it may have eventually prompted her to seek help, but alas it wasn't to be. It was by now it was fast approaching Christmas 2021 and much tougher covid rules were introduced and by the 19th December and the 21st December including the 24th December with a "stay at home warning". Christmas 2021 was thankfully shared with mum we both made the most of it. She could not understand why my son and my granddaughter could not be with

Trapped

us on Christmas day and it took a while to explain to her what the new restrictions entailed.

January and February 2022, began with heavy down pours along with very strong gusts of winds, the winds were strong eventually it destroyed some of the fence panels in my garden. The fence panels, at the time, were the talk of the village, it was only because each time there were strong winds the fence panels more than often were smashed to pieces by the strong winds. On the 22nd February 2022, I and mum took a trip in the car to the local Homebase to buy paint for the replacement fence panels along with nails. Mum thought it was wonderful to be able to venture outside having recently been couped up in the house over the Christmas and during the New Year period. We soon arrived at Homebase where I parked the car, as we got out of the car it was still very windy and I could feel the wind pushing against the door of the car, if I did not have hold of the door handles tightly the wind would have easily blown the doors wide open. The doors could have easily have hit another vehicle or person. I asked mum to wait until I came round to her side of the car so I could help her to get her out of the car. We looked around the store at the time mum asked if we could "pop" over to the local Tesco's, I agreed and as I loaded the boot of the car, with the goods we had purchased, mum was moaning about getting into the car and I asked her to wait for a moment, being such an inpatient person and at the same time I was loading the boot of the car and unbeknown to me she had managed to open the passenger door and at the time she wasn't in front of the door she was in fact stood behind the open door. All of a sudden along

Trapped

came a strong gust of wind and smashed into the door of the car. Of course mum being petite and as light as a feather, she was suddenly blown over onto the hard tarmac. As I closed the boot of the car I saw her flying in the air and then landing heavily onto the hard cold tarmac. I rushed to her side and as looked down at her left leg I could see her foot was by now facing the wrong way, I could immediately see her leg was twisted in a grotesque manner, I immediately knew she had broken her leg. At the same time she did not seem to be in any pain, the problem with mum was she had a high pain threshold and as such if anyone asked her out of 1 to 10 what level of pain she was feeling and she would reply either 1 or no pain? We had only popped out for ten minutes or so to quickly shop at Homebase I had also left my mobile at home charging up. When I saw mum laying on the tarmac I felt sick to the pit of my stomach because mum was going through so much what with her eyes and having to deal with the lockdown, and now seeing her lying helpless on the ground it was the last thing I wanted for her. Also it has to be said the country was slowly easing out of the last lockdown and it was the period of still staying within the family bubble and of course the wearing of face masks when going outside along with social distancing. Meanwhile of course I had no way of contacting 999 emergency, but luckily someone pulled up in front of me in a 4x4 and he used the vehicle to act as a windbreak. Mum was asking for me to stand her up at the same time she was complaining because she did not know what all the fuss was about, it was such a typical reaction. Meantime I took off my winter puffer jacket and I wrapped mum up to try to keep her warm as best as I possibly could. A lady pulled up in her car and

Trapped

she explained to me she was an off duty nurse I then explained about what had happened and she took one look at the position of mums leg and confirmed in her opinion it looked as though mum had in fact had broken a bone in her leg, meanwhile the driver of the 4x4 phoned 999 and I described what had happened, he then handed me the his mobile and I explained what happened in more detail and I went through answering various medical questions and passed on mums details. The operator informed me there could be a bit of a wait as the Hospitals and the ambulance services were stretched to the limit. A young lady from the Homebase store came over to mum she brought some blankets and we wrapped mum up, from the wind and the cold as best we could, mum was obviously uncomfortable having had to lay on cold tarmac I made her as comfortable as I could. I thanked everyone and of course the driver of the 4x4 for his assistance. I would never come out of the house without my mobile again. Eventually an ambulance turned up and the paramedic team reviewed mums condition one of the paramedics confirmed mum had indeed broken her left leg it and looked to them as though she had broken her left femur. They gently got her onto a trolley and it is when mum called out "Keith where are they taking me, please don't tell me I have to go to hospital, please I don't want to go to any hospital"? I walked with her to the ambulance and the paramedics the loaded the trolley onto the ambulance. I was allowed into the ambulance and wearing my face mask, I was asked many questions including mum's overall health and if she was allergic to any medicines and what type of medication was she taking at the time. One of the paramedics once again asked mum if she was in any pain, she replied "no not at all apart from you lot wasting your time". He replied "Mrs Hearn we believe you have broken your left leg, now do you require anything to numb the pain"? she replied "no thank you". The other paramedic had by now finished hooking her up to various pieces of equipment and informed me they would be taking mum to Basingstoke hospital as the local Hospital did not operate on patients with such a break. I asked if I could stay with mum inside the ambulance but sadly I was informed I could not travel with her as the A&E Dept at Basingstoke was in total COVID-19 lockdown and was only accessible to patients. I explained to mum I could not stay with her she would have to travel to Basingstoke Hospital on her own, poor mum she had a look of total shock on her face, the colour had by now once again drained from her face, she panicked and told the para medics she wanted to get out of the ambulance only because if I could not go with her to hospital she was refusing to be taken to the hospital, it took a while to calm her, it could have been the shock setting in, I don't know, but throughout the many times she has had to attend hospital more so since my dad had passed away, I have always been with her. On this occasion I couldn't follow in my car because I would not have been able to enter the A&E Dept or to visit her on the ward due to the COVID rules. I watched as the ambulance left the car park with blue lights flashing I continued to watch as it joined the motorway and headed in the direction of Basingstoke. The area around my car was eerily quiet I looked at the car and I could see the passenger door was still wide open. What turned out to be a ten minute "pop" to the local Homebase had ended up as being an accident scene and almost two hours

Trapped

later mum had broken her leg and she was by now being rushed to hospital. As they say "Never a Dull Moment".

I drove home and as I opened the door to the house and as I stepped inside it seemed so quiet I put the shopping away and picked up my mobile phone to speak to my brothers Michael and Garry and I informed them of what had recently happened to mum. Later the same evening I received a call from the hospital informing me, mum had recently had undergone major surgery on her left femur and a metal rod was inserted into the bone to help close the break. She was to be moved on to a ward sometime in the early morning and I was informed she was well and was holding up fine, the caller mentioned she was somewhat of a strong character and she had been asking for me. I asked when would I be able to visit her, I was informed I would need to contact the admissions team the following morning. Once again I updated my brothers regarding her operation and mum was to be moved onto a ward sometime in the early morning, obviously they asked if I could update them as and when I received more information regarding our mums condition.

The following morning I contacted the admissions team at the hospital and I was informed of the ward mum had been moved to, I obtained the contact number and quickly phoned the ward, where someone then informed me that I could not visit mum, only because she was still recovering from the post operation but I could visit the following day, but I must phone before 11 am because of the COVID restrictions I must phone so the ward staff could book me in for a visit and at the time the visits were for one hour only and no longer. I was disappointed but at the same time I understood and if mum was awake she would have expected me to have visited and no matter how she was feeling I was in the hands of the hospital and things were difficult and because of the COVID restrictions within all hospitals. The following day I travelled to the hospital I soon found the ward and obviously I had to wear a mask and to clean my hands before accessing the ward, I got to the ward doors and found they were locked so I rang a bell and a nurse met me at the door I was taken to the wards reception desk where a nurse checked to see if I had in fact booked a visit. I was then taken to a side ward where mum was sat up in bed and as I walked into her ward she instantly spotted me, I think she may have been watching the entrance to the ward for hours, her eyes widened and had a large smile on her face I could tell straight away she was very happy to see me. I gave her a hug along with a kiss, I had some bags containing her toiletries and dressing gown also her night dresses and of course her nice fluffy slippers. The first thing she said was "Keith I am dying of thirst could you please get me a cup of tea". Of course I could not just go and make her a cup of tea so I asked a nurse if she could arrange for a cup of tea, a nice cup of tea soon arrived. Mum and I had a long chat and once again I informed her she could not go back home of course more so since having broken her leg, she shocked me she agreed to stay with me, I felt relieved because she hadn't screamed the ward down or argued with me. I was then handed some administration paper work, the person who handed me the paper work informed me as they found mum did not know any of the information, anyway the nurse told me mum kept saying was "wait until Keith gets here and he will fill it in".

Trapped

Anyway I duly filled in the form and I wrote down my address and my contact details on the form I was asked where mum would be living post release from the hospital once again I wrote down my address. The hour was soon up I said my goodbyes and asked mum if she wanted me to bring anything specific with me during the next visit the following day. She said "only you Keith", I looked at her and gave her a peck on the cheek, she looked terrified sat in bed, I also think she was somewhat confused I was not surprised. I left her I felt so sorry for her only because her feisty spirit seemed to have all but disappeared. I drove home to Winchester with lots of thoughts rushing through my head and I had more questions than answers. It did not help due to the COVID restrictions within the hospital to only having one hour visiting time, but it was the system in place at the time and it was in place for the safety of the patients, I believe at the time one of the wards was completely closed to all visitors due to an outbreak of the COVID virus. At the time every visitor to the hospital had to have a clear lateral flow test visitors and would have to bring the lateral flow strip to the hospital to prove a test had been taken and to prove it was negative, I was never asked for proof. At the time I thought anyone who wasn't as honest could have so easily have used a lateral flow test which was negative and wasn't in fact theirs. I fully understood why visitors were required to carry out lateral flow tests. As soon as I returned home, there was a phone call from the hospital it was a doctor who wanted to speak to me regarding mums mental health. He was summoned by the ward staff, where mum was being cared for they were concerned about mums state of mind and he informed me he had carried out some basic memory tests, apparently he was not happy at all and he wanted to inform me. He told me mum had failed the basic memory tests, I informed him of the history of the memory tests she had undergone in Swindon, at the same time matter of the memory tests had been surpassed by the pandemic and I had been side tracked by mums double cataract operations. He went on to tell me the hospital would have to inform her GP of what has happened, regarding the hospitals findings. I informed him about mum was in fact living with me and I gave him the Gratton Surgery contact details in Winchester. I went on to inform him if I had been able to travel with mum to the A&E department I would have been able to explain all about my mums mental health. He was happy with what I told him of course I could not just turn around and visit mum on the ward, to help to reassure her and to help calm her. After the hospital memory clinic team having questioned her and having carried out some tests, I knew instinctively she would have been very confused, upset and scared, about as she would call it, being placed into a nut house. The tests were carried out without the assurance I would be with her, I pointed this out to the doctor. He informed me he would contact mums GP in Winchester for a referral to the community mental health team and for a cognition assessment.

I booked myself in for a visit the following day at the hospital and I was informed I would need to phone back the following morning and it must be before 11 am for me to be able to book a slot for me to visit the ward, I could only book on the day of the visit and to then drive to Basingstoke to visit by 11 am. On the second day of the visit to the wards the physio team were standing around her bed also at the side of her bed there was a wipe board, with mums name on it along with the date and who was visiting her on a daily basis of course my details were written on the board. One of the physiotherapists said to me they were very pleased with mums progress, and once again I was asked who was going to look after mum whenever she was eventually discharged from the hospital, I once again gave my address and my contact telephone numbers. The physio explained to me my mum was more than eager to get back onto her feet, but as it was only day two since her operation she was told she needed to remain in bed for a little bit longer. The physio's left as I was talking to mum she suddenly showed me her broken leg, my gosh it was very badly bruised actually I was not that surprised having recently broken her femur and having undergone a major operation and to have a metal rod inserted through the top of the femur to help to provide support to her left leg. Mind you mum's mind set was as she explained to me "Keith they said if I can get around in a wheel chair and if I can move on my own with the help of a Zimmer frame they will have no option but to let me go home" I replied "yes mum but all in good time, not on day two", she scowled at me. We had a chat regarding her having to stay with me to help her to recover, I said "if you tell the medical staff you are going to be staying at your bungalow all on your own in Swindon I am afraid you will be on your own, the hospital will have to inform social services in Swindon and for them to find social accommodation for you, so the choice is yours or the other option is to stay with me or be looked after by social services"? She got the point and at the time she never once mentioned her recent memory test, I suppose it was bad enough having recently having broken her leg. I did not raise the issue of the memory test or the results. I knew full well the hospital memory clinic team would be in contact with either her GP or the community mental health team.

There was one day I had to explain to mum I needed to get somethings done at home and I had to work that particular day. Luckily my brother Garry said he would visit mum and it was a relief and mum would have another one of her sons to be with her. During my visits to the hospital the physiotherapy team would inform me of how well mum was doing and one morning when I arrived at the hospital mum wasn't in her bed and I asked a nurse if all was ok regarding mum, the nurse smiled and she told me my mum was flying around the ward on a Zimmer frame, at that moment she was in the toilet, low and behold I heard her distinctive loud scouse voice. There she was whizzing into the ward with the help of a Zimmer frame of course when she saw me she was laughing her head off, I looked surprised only because after having only recently gone through a major operation and here she was on her feet and walking around the ward, albeit with the help of a frame. When the visit was over I quickly made a phone call to my son Paul and asked him to order a double bed, I would pay him the next time I saw him, I explained about how his gran was back on her feet and she was using a frame to get around, I said if she was progressing so quickly it then would not be too long before the, hospital team would discharge her from hospital. I also realised mum would not be able to get up and down the stairs to her B&B bedroom, even though she was doing so well whizzing around the hospital ward one of the physios said to me it seemed as though mums nasty fall had by now rapidly brought on further signs of dementia, I pointed out no one had yet confirmed she had dementia, because mum hadn't had a CT scan confirming a diagnoses of dementia and on one of the days when I was visiting the ward a doctor came to visit mum and before he got to mum's bed a physio took him to the side where they spoke in length with him. The doctor then asked me if I could pop out of the ward where he apologised for the physio having mentioned mum may have dementia. I told him it was OK as I only wanted the truth and I also wanted to know what to expect once she came home to live with me. He said the operation to fix her femur was a huge success but she did in fact showed signs of suffering with a form of dementia, he said "you don't seem to be surprised Mr Hearn"? I replied "no not really I would like to know are you now confirming she has dementia"? He replied "no that question would need to be answered by the community mental health team", he also pointed out mum was incontinent. At home I knew she was always running to the toilet and he mentioned a lot of elderly people do have things happen to them and more so after a nasty fall/broken bones, the dementia may have taken a turn for the worse. I returned to mum where the doctor explained to her she was making excellent progress and she would be home soon, he asked her if she had any questions for him and of course she didn't but I could tell her mind was working overtime and of course I knew why. Her first question to me was "well Keith go and ask someone when I can come home please" I then walked over to the nurses reception area to ask when would it be before mum could return home and I was told it could be sometime during the coming weekend.

During mums physiotherapy the physiotherapist's informed me mum would not be able to go home in the car only because her femur was repairing itself and by getting in and out of my car it could so easily cause serious damage to her leg and they explained to me, she would in fact be returning home in hospital transport. As I was travelling to and from hospital on a daily basis I didn't have time to purchase food or new bedding for mums new bed and I hadn't yet sorted where she was going to sleep at night, luckily the bathroom and toilet is downstairs in my house and it was one positive thing. Myself and my son Paul soon converted the conservatory into a bedroom including a small living room for mum. To be honest it looked very comfortable and because I am not very good at putting furniture together but my son is very good and of course he had the right tools to quickly put the bed together, between the pair of us it did not take very long to get the bedroom room ready. Mum was discharged over the coming weekend and she arrived home in hospital transport, she was in a wheel chair the crew managed to get her inside the living room and left me with the discharge documentation, medicine, along with her spare clothes and a Zimmer frame. I thanked them for bringing her home they soon had to leave to drop off yet another patient at their home, the first thing mum said to me was "someone could die of thirst" and burst out laughing, she was so relieved to be home. Just prior to mum having been discharged from the hospital I purchased a Zimmer frame of our own along with a stool along with handles as I thought it would help her sit at the bathroom sink where she would be able to wash herself and clean her teeth. The same afternoon I watched mum try to get around the house I could see she was going to struggle getting herself around the house. The first evening mum slept inside the conservatory and I turned on two heaters to ensure the room was warm enough for whenever she went to bed. I got her to use the Zimmer frame to help to get herself more mobile whenever she tried to walk around the living room and the kitchen area, it took a bit of time to get her into the conservatory as soon as I soon had her tucked up in bed I gave her a kiss on the forehead. She seemed pleased with the room of course with the new bed including the bedding. I said good night to her and then went upstairs to my bed. I dropped off to sleep but alas it wasn't long before I was woken by the sound of mum crying, just prior to going to sleep I opened my bedroom window so I could hear whenever mum was awake and she was moving around, I also kept the living room door open once again so I could hear if mum somehow had managed to get herself out of bed. Mum suffered with childhood nightmares and so when I heard her crying I thought it was because she was having "one of her nightmares". I could hear her calling out my name and I quickly rushed downstairs where I almost tripped over my trainers I left on the stairs. I rushed into the conservatory and tried my best to reassure her everything was going to be alright, I switched on the bedside lamp I could see my poor mum was very upset and tears were running down her face. She explained to me she thought she was in her words "I thought I was still inside that horrible hospital all on my own", She asked if I could help take her to the bathroom, I manged to get her out of bed as I did

Trapped

so I could see she had an accident, she was embarrassed more so because I am her son and she felt I should not see her in such a state. I explained to her all was ok and for her not to worry as soon as I got her to the bathroom she took her wet night clothes off and managed to wash herself, I knocked on the bathroom door and I slipped some clean nightclothes through the door and I stripped her bed and washed the mattress then turned it over it was then I realised I needed to purchase a mattress cover and in the meantime I used portable heaters to dry the mattress. It was very lucky I had a washing machine along with a tumble dryer as the weather during the time was constantly raining. With mum staying with me and having accidents and as such I would never have got the washing dry without a tumble dryer. This was only the beginning of the journey of caring for mum it was a taste of what was to come. When mum came into the living room she was once again upset more so because of her accident and having placed yet more work onto my shoulders, I told her it was OK and I just needed to put some routines in place such as buying two mattress covers, extra night clothes, along with more bedding. I helped to sit her down onto the couch and of course I then made a nice cup of tea along with some biscuits, after she calmed down she said "hey Keith I can get used to this, waking up in the morning being spoilt with cups of tea and biscuits". We both laughed and I replied "hey this isn't a hotel you know" we laughed. I managed to get her back to bed and the washing was on the go throughout the night. The following working day I contacted the surgery regarding mums accident and her GP replied she may well be incontinent, a District Nurse was due to visit the same week to check on mums leg and to provide some

Trapped

physio exercises for her to do on her own. Anyway it was time for the District Nurse to visit the house, it was at this stage I picked up mum did not want anyone to visit the house, I explained I would be with her whenever the nurses were visiting the house, I noticed she became somewhat distressed, she had never been like this in the past, for me it was something new. The nurse duly arrived and he checked mums blood pressure pulse etc and he also checked mums leg also took a look at the scar on her leg and he commented "oh that's a very neat scar". Mum laughed and then said "I wish I did not need to have the operation, if it wasn't for my son I would never have had the operation" the nurse looked at me and said "that's a very strange thing to say Mrs Hearn". He asked me some questions regarding how mum was managing to get around the house also about her daily hygiene routine, he asked her to walk around the living room and then into the kitchen using the Zimmer frame. She completed the task and sat back down on the couch he asked if he could have a chat in the kitchen as he spoke he said "your mum is shuffling her feet and she is not picking them up", I mentioned I did notice she was walking like that prior to her recent fall, he replied the hospital had in fact recorded they thought she had all of the classic signs of Dementia. The shuffling was one of the signs of dementia along with so many other signs. Regarding the incontinence it was advisable to purchase incontinence pants it would help mum and myself, because I was her full time carer and would have to clean up after each "accident".

During the visit she overheard the word dementia and she let rip with both the nurse and myself, she vehemently denied there was anything wrong with her and she was not a "nutter" I managed to calm her. The nurse soon left the house and before he left he apologised for letting slip regarding the dementia aspect of mums health, I told him not to worry about it, I explained mum was in somewhat of a denial mode and it was understandable, as no one wants to hear those fearful words dementia.

I went online where I ten ordered some incontinence pants for mum, I wanted to buy nice ones so she would not feel awkward, the pants arrived and they may have looked "normal" but they did not do the job, I purchased other makes and they also did not do the job. One day I mentioned the pant issue to my next door neighbour Maria and she mentioned to me Tesco's own and so I purchased a pack they may not look frilly and nice but my goodness they were perfect and of course they also did the job. By now I was using mattress covers in case there was ever a leak, the odd time there were leaks and of course mums night clothes became wet but not as much as the early days. I soon decided to stick to the Tesco's pants right up until mums sad demise.

I contacted her GP and I informed him I had noticed a massive change in mums mental health since having her accident and breaking her leg, he pointed out to me some people who are suffering with any form of dementia, would eventually plateau and somewhat stabilise but seemingly if they have had a massive trauma such as mum's broken leg their mental health takes somewhat of a dive once again it seems to plateau at a lower/next level. It was at this point after mum was discharged from the hospital I began to notice a decline in her health along with major changes in her mental health. I have to say I began to research as much as I could online regarding dementia along with its affects, I know it is often said not to use the internet regarding health issues but at the time I felt because the hospital and the nurses were by now dropping into the conversation the word dementia and at the time I felt I needed to find out as much as I could about all aspects of the disease, to help prepare both mum and I to what to expect. As I initially searched for information and the many reasons and causes of dementia popped up on my laptop screen and two words stood out they were dementia and Alzheimer's, the words filled me with so much dread. Much has been written regarding people who are suffering with the disease and falling over due to a lack of balance, I wondered if it may have been the cause to mum having recently falling over in the car park, but there again my logical thoughts were because it happened all due to a strong gust of wind and mum having been hit by the car door? A few weeks after she was discharged from the hospital and very soon afterwards I received a phone call from the dementia team within Winchester because mum was still recovering from her recent fall and she was only able to get round with a frame, she would never be able to get in and out of my car and so it was arranged for a mental health nurse to visit the house. After the call I was in a catch 22 situation as I could not bluntly say to mum "oh by the way a mental health nurse will be popping round to the house to see you", only because mum would have gone mad, I could not let someone just turn up out of the blue without explaining who or when someone was going to visit mum. So it was I told her, a nurse would be visiting the house to see how she was getting on after her recent operation. Her reply was "god Keith how many more people are going to

Trapped

visit the house to see me"? Her words were poetic only because as her dementia was becoming so much worse we would see lots of people visiting the house. It was by now the day a nurse was coming to visit mum and examine mum. When she arrived she explained everything she was going also what she was going to ask mum, my mum was none the wiser and said "you will have to explain to Keith, as to what is going to happen, I am not very good with technical medical questions" I went on to explain to her, about the questions the nurse was going to ask and mum would need to answer on her own as I could not answer the questions for her, it was yet another memory test and this one would be far more specific, than the one undertaken by her GP in Swindon and it would be more along the lines as the one she undertook at the Great Western Hospital memory clinic. During the normal medical questions and of course the memory questions, I immediately knew mum had drastically failed the test. Even though mum kept asking me for the answers to the questions and sadly I could not help her, it was heart wrenching to hear her struggle with the questions.

As the nurse left the house and as we stood in the garden, I said to her "look I know my mum has failed the memory test, what happens next", She was honest with me and she confirmed with me mum had not done very well. From the initial results she was displaying all of the classic dementia and/or Alzheimer's signs, she could not be more specific, a consultant would have to review the results of the test and would be informing the specialist with my observations. The next stage would be an appointment for a CT scan on her brain to see if there had been any damage, if any damage was found the team should be able to gauge how much damage has been done. It was around the same time and bearing in mind my mum was highly likely to have dementia, I had to broach the subject of where mum was going to live, my thoughts along with my brothers. It was very obvious, to myself, she could no longer look after herself at home and I could not keep driving back and forward to Swindon and at this point she was still paying rent, fuel bills including the council tax on a property she was no longer living in. I am afraid it was like lighting the blue touch paper of a fire work. Let's say she was angry and very unhappy at the thought of having to give up her bungalow. During the period of her recuperation from the surgery on her left femur, she was becoming extremely argumentative and was becoming somewhat verbally aggressive towards myself, I have to stress there was never any physical violence towards me. There was a massive change of character, yes she was always feisty and had a sharp tongue but at this stage this was a totally different side of her character it was a change which would remain with her until the end of her life. I sometimes did not know what person would turn up whenever I woke up and it was becoming obvious mum was changing and at times I do not think she knew what was going on around her.

As soon as mum was well enough and she was ready to place some weight on to the left leg and without the aid of a frame. I was able to get her in and out of the car once again she was by now biting at the bit for me to take her home to her bungalow, to collect her post and check her bungalow. As soon as we arrived at the bungalow, her next door neighbour saw my car was parked outside of the bungalow he knocked on the back door, he was invited into the living room he spoke to mum for a length of time. One thing I did not want him to do and it was to mention anything to do with dementia as he already knew about the possibility of mum having dementia because mum had previously mentioned during the past also she had mentioned to him having to visit the memory clinic. But of course he whittled on about how the disease eats away at the brain I could tell that mum was somewhat confused by now I could tell she was about to blow her top, I politely asked him to leave the bungalow. He left and then there was another knock on the back door this time and it was her other next door neighbour Jenny. Mum was very pleased to see her they had a long chat about mums front garden, mum was so proud of her garden, the talk soon turned to what mum had missed in the neighbourhood and of course there was plenty of gossip, Jenny then left as it was time for mum and I to return to Winchester. It was difficult to persuade her to get into the car because it was her bungalow of course she sorely missed her life and her neighbours. As always we took the route via Marlborough as it was handy to pop into Tesco's and for mum to use the toilets. Prior to mum having been diagnosed with Dementia and Alzheimer's I tried hard for mum to agree to hand back her bungalow to Swindon Council. I am afraid things always ended up with an argument only because mum was a proud and independent person also somewhat of a battler, a true fighter, so far I held off from handing back the bungalow. Many times I spoke to my brothers regarding the bungalow and they agreed with me mum should move out of her place and move in with me.

Trapped

There was another point, it may seem like a minor point, but for me it was becoming a major issue, it was becoming more difficult to get her in and out of the car as she became less mobile. On one of our trips she somehow managed to gauge one of her legs along a piece of plastic inside of the car it had ripped the skin from one of her legs and caused a rather nasty gash, it took a long time to heal due to her blood circulation issues. The car and mums leg looked as though there had been a major accident. There was blood everywhere of course it covered her leg and the passenger side of the car.

Over time she became more aggressive and somewhat angry at me only because she got it into her head I was trying to make excuses to why she could not go home. Lockdown had by now came and went we were so lucky not to have succumbed to the dreaded COVID pandemic, I don't know how we did it, but we did. I will return to the time mum was recuperating from the operation on her femur, I was trying my hardest to get her to walk and with the use of the Zimmer frame it was an absolute nightmare, because at this point she developed a habit of putting all of her weight onto one side of the frame of course the frame would become unbalanced I could see she was going to topple over, so I would stop her and ask her to take her time to take smaller steps. Once again she hadn't yet been officially diagnosed with dementia or for that matter Alzheimer's.
At the time mum would often become frustrated due to her inability to walk to the Littleton stud and at times she would become verbally aggressive, I could understand why she was frustrated at having been kept indoors during the lockdowns of

course she was by now struggling to overcome and mend after the operation on her leg, I noticed whenever she was verbally aggressive, the following day she would not remember anything about the arguments. Of course it was becoming obvious the dementia was taking a strong hold. It was such an awful situation for mum, at times she could not remember the arguments and she often did not know who I was. As I was the one who was watching her decline in her health, it was an awful situation to be in. Whenever I mentioned to her about how she was reacting to me, she became upset and of course I could tell she was very worried, but she would not admit she was worried I am afraid it was mum all over.

Within the family mum was well known as being somewhat of "a sun goddess", at my house I have a lean to glass conservatory attached to the side of the house. At first I would place a kitchen chair inside of the conservatory it allowed mum to sun bath, it was a big mistake only because the chair had no arms for her to lean on. It was a huge mistake to let mum sunbathe on that particular chair without any arms to support her. It was because the longer she had to wait for a diagnoses for dementia her balance was becoming so much worse and was noticeable. One afternoon I was working in the rear garden where I thought I could keep an eye on her and to ensure she was safe, all went quite, it was unusual because mum was continuously talking or shouting. I then looked up to see where she was I could just about make out she was laid out on the hard conservatory floor, I immediately ran towards the conservatory my stomach seemed to do summersaults I entered the conservatory when mum said

Trapped

"don't just stand there get me up" I replied "no mum not yet I have to make sure you haven't damaged your femur or broken any bones". I checked her over and luckily I could tell she hadn't broken anything also there was no blood. I was going to phone 999 but mum assured me she was in fact was ok, it took a while to get her onto the chair and slowly walked her into the living room where I made her comfortable and made her a sweet cup of tea along with a piece of her favourite cake. I switched on the TV I found a comedy film from the sixties for her to watch.. At the same time I popped outside and I contacted my brothers to let them know what had happened to mum and to keep them informed. As I walked into the living room she shouted at me "there you go again telling tales about me, I want to go home" Once again I had a rough night's sleep, I had been woken as usual during the early hours of the morning I was up and about having changed mums night clothes. After cleaning herself and dressing her in clean clothing and of course the washing machine was whirling away, I made a cup of tea for both of us once again we had a nice slice of cake, I mentioned to her about accusing me of being a telltale and once again she could not remember anything about what she had said to me. She also could not remember having fallen over, she did say she vaguely remembered that something had happened what it was she hadn't a clue. It was during this period things were happening more frequently. Mum would fight with me, pushing against anything I was trying to do for her, such as caring for her and trying my very best to make life so much easy for her. Everyone in the family knew of mums childhood and she would sometimes lapse into her childhood memories and she would tell me about what her childhood was

Trapped

like and her memories seemed to have sometimes blurred into what was currently happening to her. All I ever wanted for her was for her to let me look after her and for her to enjoy her life whenever she stayed with me.

Chapter 3 – Shocking News

During April 2022 I messaged my brothers informing them of how I was getting on with mum also to let them know how I was getting on both mentally and physically, I pointed out to them just how physically exhausting it was looking after our mum, I also pointed out I was not complaining I was only pointing out, how draining it was, not having a decent night sleep and having to tidy up after mum for example changing her bedding twice a night and also changing her nightclothes.

There were times when I came home from my part time job only to find her having soaked the couch and was sadly still be sat in her wet clothes, poor mum, I would often find the living room carpet soaked through. These were the early days of caring for her and I was still learning about caring for someone who at the time was suffering with dementia.

Also, an added issue at the time was her incontinence and her GP was somewhat reluctant to prescribe any medication to assist with her incontinence, it was because he was trying to diagnose her other medical issues she was suffering from at the time. He was by now aware her red blood cells were not producing enough oxygen in her blood. He took her off some of her previous medication and prescribed Iron tablets, once she had taken enough of the Iron tablets, she would then be taken off the tablets to undergo more blood tests, and at this time her blood pressure was normal and there was nothing to worry about. At the same time, she was able to walk without the aid of a Zimmer frame.

Trapped

Towards the end of April 2022 I informed my brothers Michael and Garry, about how I had once again found mum sprawled out on the ground, she had once again fallen over, as I was checking her to ensure she hadn't broken any of her bones, I could see she had blood oozing from her knees and she wasn't able to get herself up from off the ground. I noticed her clothes also had gravel covering her skirt and it made me feel she had been walking outside of the conservatory. At this point I did not know how much damage the dementia was doing to her and I have to be honest I had no idea how rapid the dementia could destroy someone's mind, plus I think at the time I did not want mum to be suffering with such a horrible disease. I tried talking to mum about her having fallen over and getting up to mischief whenever I was not around. What I got instead was an aggressive mother who was in denial regarding her falls. At times the falls made me feel sick to the stomach and it was very upsetting to see my frail mum sprawled on the ground, no one wants to see an elderly parent hurting themselves even more so when they have fallen over and for no apparent reason, I felt horrified for her, at this point she could not explain what happened to her. She would often throw everything I was trying to do for her back in my face. Of course at this time most of my messages to my brothers may have seemed to them as though I was continuously moaning, yes at times I was down having to look after mum, I have to say without being able to "let off steam" to my brothers may have been somewhat of an issue regarding my own health. Do not get me wrong, looking after mum was not a bed of roses, but by letting off steam to my brothers, was nothing compared to what was happening to our mum, I was so scared of the unknown. So, God only knows how my mum was feeling?

Trapped

During the same April I once again contacted mums GP with many questions regarding her health. Bearing in mind as a family we had not yet had a diagnosis of dementia, it looked as though she in fact had the classic signs of having the disease.

When I contacted her GP I pointed out the many issues regarding her mental state it did and as though my mum was suffering from the early onset of Alzheimer's or Dementia, or perhaps at this point and unknown to me she was in fact battling with advanced dementia.

I informed her GP of my following observations:
My mum was waking up throughout the night due to her incontinence and she was having to wear incontinence pants. At the same time, she was becoming increasingly disoriented and very weak and was argumentative.

Her symptoms meant I was having to get up to assist my mum and I would have a disturbed night's sleep. I am a diabetic and my own GP was monitoring diabetes. I wanted to also point out I was not complaining, and I pointed out I need to be fit and well to be able to help my mum. I realised the NHS system was/is under great strain and there was a backlog of patients who needed to be seen or assessed at most hospitals within the UK.

At the time, the information I had in my possession was contained within the various handbooks and the various leaflets left by the NHS agencies. Whenever they visited the house, of course there was a lot more information online, I would only go online to look at the information regarding dementia and Alzheimer's on the NHS, Dementia Society, and the Alzheimer's web pages.

Trapped

When a nurse from the local NHS "Pro Active Care Team" visited the house. She carried out a myriad of tests and gave me some contact details and as I have mentioned leaflets for me to help guide me to get the support available to me. It was found mums weight had dropped to 7st 2 pounds. Also, her blood pressure was somewhat on the low side. Mum then undertook the memory test, and she failed, no surprises there, out of a score of 28 she had only scored 2. The nurse then asked mum to walk from the living room and into the kitchen, she was concerned mum was shuffling and she was not walking properly. It was something I previously noticed, and I had updated her surgery. The nurse let mum ramble on, and it was soon apparent, mum was just rambling, and she was not making much sense she went on to blame me for getting the nurse to see her when there was nothing wrong with her health?? The nurse gently put mum straight and informed her why she was visiting the house. When a district nurse first visited the house, not long after she had been discharged from hospital after breaking her leg, it was the first time anyone had pointed out to me. My mum was shuffling when she was walking.

My main thought at the time were what will happen after the visit? The nurse would be submitting a report to the surgery regarding the results of the memory test. She went onto explain about how my mum would be referred to a specialist for an appointment to have a CT scan. There are no drugs which would slow down the Dementia. I mentioned the times mum had fallen over; the Nurse explained to me it was a common side effect of what was going on. She told mum during the visit it was a time to be open and honest. There is a motion alarm, and she was going to submit a request for me to have one for free if not it would cost £20 a month. There would also be a follow up visit by another

Trapped

nurse who would take mums bloods and to check for her B12 and her folic acid levels. I was informed her weight loss was a side effect of dementia and the nurse asked me to begin to give mum protein drinks. As mentioned previously my mum did not like the taste of the protein drinks and refused to drink them. The nurse asked me not to contact the Memory team in Winchester, because her thorough report would be the "kick start" for the NHS system to action the findings of her visit as mum had only scored only 2 on the memory test and there would be a higher sense of urgency.

One morning I managed to complete some writing in the garden shed at @10 am as soon as I finished writing I came into the house. Where mum seemed once again to be agitated and I asked her if everything was OK, she replied no and went on to tell me "that woman has stolen all of my clothes" it was a figure of her imagination, I reassured her everything was OK and I did not want to go through this again, because things were by now slowly wearing me down. I count myself as a very patient person, there is a limit as to what anyone can take. After calming her and as usual I put a film on the TV then made her a nice cup of tea and of course a slice of cake, I decided to go to bed for an hours sleep, if I could catch an hour or so of sleep after having a disturbed and broken night's sleep, I could face a full day of caring for mum.
Later, during this particular day it was early afternoon, and I was trying to carry out some gardening, mum was sat outside in the conservatory and once again she was looking agitated and somewhat angry. I asked her if everything was OK, it was then she said, "no I am not, you bloody hit me, and you were also shouting at me". By this point I was in a state of shock, I could not believe what she had said to me. I immediately contacted my younger brother Garry, and I explained to him what mum had

said. He spoke to mum, and she was able to tell him what she thought had happened, after he finished speaking to mum, he told me mum seemed very confused and tired, he advised me to try and walk away from any confrontational scenes. Later the same afternoon, she attempted to lock me indoors and took the key from out of the lock to the back door and then placed the key on the outside and attempted to turn the key in the outer lock, I noticed what she was trying to do and quickly took the key from her. From that time onwards I would take a spare key for the front door along with a back door key with me at all times. Normally after an hour or so mum seemed to be back to something of her old self. But the mood swings and verbal outbursts became more frequent. Unknown to me at times mum was able to get herself out of bed and to get to the toilet unaided, it was a surprise to me only because at this time she was very weak and frail. It is amazing what someone can do at times.

Sometimes she would shout my name from the bottom of the stairs, informing me it was time to get up for work, even though it was 3 or 4 o'clock in the morning. At times I would come downstairs only to find mum had once again fallen over. One morning I found her in the living room where she had somehow shuffled along on her bottom from having fallen outside. Because of her fall she could not get herself up from off the floor. Once again, I was shocked; to see her on the floor in so much distress, it was so heart wrenching to see her suffering. As I helped her to her feet, she had once again verbally attacked me and once again threatened to go back home, this was not going to happen as she was incapable of looking after herself. I did point out to her if she continued to ignore what I was saying to her, she would once again end up breaking a leg, this time she might not be able to walk again, as her recent broken leg was a very serious break.

Trapped

She was upset at what I had said to her, I think it was more so because she once again had done her own thing and because of it, the fall was the consequence. At the same time, I was still treating one of her knees after her latest fall. She was not happy when I told her I would be informing my brothers of her latest fall once again she began arguing with me. She spouted such things as "you will not need to worry about me, when I am dead". I informed her she was being very naughty by saying such things. At the time my number one concern was her unseen illness and by now it seemed have escalated to yet another level. She had never accused me of hitting her in the past. Things hadn't been very good at the time and by now I was on my last week of the fortnight off work. I was in somewhat of a state of shock having been accused by mum of hitting her, I have to say I obviously knew it was down to the effects of the dementia and at the time it must have seemed like she was living through a nightmare.

It was soon time for her to have her B12 booster jab during this period we had the local fire brigade home visit, it is something the NHS team who were looking after mum had recommended. While they were visiting the house we had some new smoke alarms fitted. One of the team was sat with mum in the living room and I could hear them talking to mum, I took the other member of the team upstairs where they then fitted some smoke alarms, and a carbon monoxide alarm situated close to the boiler. When I came downstairs the fire officer who was talking to mum had recommended to me mum was not to touch the oven, it was after she asked mum some basic safety questions, they weren't at all happy with her answers to the questions. The fire officer confirmed due to mums' mental health state, and it was recommended she should never be around the oven; it was for her own safety. The fire officers confirmed with Hampshire

Trapped

County Council of the visit also the installing of the fire alarms along with the carbon monoxide monitor. They would be adding a recommendation, and it was my mum should not be allowed near the oven.

She was becoming very moody during the daytime. Once again, she had thought a woman was stealing her clothes, I was aware of what this imaginary woman was up to. Mum at the time did not know what was going on around her and I am afraid things were becoming so much worse. One summer evening she came into the garden I could see one of her fingers was pouring with blood, I found out she had used a sharp pair of paper scissors to cut her nails. Hence more arguments and I am afraid to say it was one sided. I sat her down within the living room where I wrapped her badly cut finger in tissue paper, Luckily, I had plenty of dressings and some tcp and cream. By now she was panicking because she thought she would have to go to the local hospital. When I had finished cleaning and dressing her finger, we had a nice cup of tea. The following morning, she did not have a clue as to what happened to her finger. She could not remember having cut it with a pair of scissors. I had to "hide" all scissors from her to ensure she did not cut her fingers or any other area on her body.

It was by now approaching the end of August 2022 once again I made contact with her GP by now he was fully aware of my mums medical condition/s and at this stage things had not improved, it was more than likely over the long term her condition would become so much worse?
I reminded him regarding one of the nurses who recently visited my home where she carried out various checks on mum, one of these was a memory test, my mum only scored 2 out of 28. I informed him of the results of the checkup along with the recent

memory test score and eventually a report would be sent to the surgery. Recently mum had once again had her B12 jab. Vitamin B12 injections are given to prevent or treat vitamin B12 deficiency. B12 is a vital nutrient which helps make DNA and haemoglobin. The jabs are usually administered to people with absorption issues or those who have undergone gastric surgery. They may also reduce the risk of developing certain health disorders, including neurological conditions. In mums case it was because of Vascular Dementia and Alzheimer's.

I knew at the same time the NHS system was and still is at breaking point and there would inevitably be delays in the system. Mums' general health, mentally and physically, was deteriorating. She did not seem to recognise other members of her own family, such as my brothers or any of her grandchildren or great-grandchildren. It was time to once again to contact her GP and as I have mentioned my mother's major fall and the subsequent operation to pin her left femur. Since having fallen over she had not been herself. She was by now shuffling as she walked, her brain was telling her she could walk correctly, but physically it was not happening. All due to the recent and nasty break to her leg. Her incontinence also prevented her from leaving the house or going for long walks.

Her mind was stuck on a Thursday, even though I purchased a dementia clock. On many occasions she informed me she was not very hungry, i.e., such as first thing in the morning. I would sit with her at mealtimes just to make sure she was eating the food I had placed in front of her. At the time, her weight was below seven stone. I was informed by the various NHS agencies I was saving the NHS a small

Trapped

fortune regarding looking after my mum at home hence freeing up hospital beds etc. At the time everyone in my family was extremely concerned about the rapid decline in mum's health.

Chapter 4 – Mums Demise

I desperately needed answers and as such I laid out a few points for mum's GP to think about such as whether there was going to be further medical follow-ups regarding the obvious onset of Alzheimer's/Dementia. I had questions to which I needed some answers such as, was it too late to offer her further treatment to avert the further onset of dementia? Would she require a specialist appointment for more assessments? Would she require a scan to ascertain how much damage her brain had suffered? Did I need to wait for the surgery to direct me as to what happens next if so, what was the lead time to getting something in place for her? Would the surgery inform me if there was nothing more to be done for mum or for things to take their natural course?
At the time I felt as though I needed to have a far better understanding of mum's treatment or the lack of further treatment. I had to remind the surgery I was not a trained mental nurse also I certainly did not have the experience or the knowledge as to what was going to happen long term regarding her health. At that moment, I felt as though I had been parachuted in to help care for my mum when in fact I had been dropped into a minefield, along with the consequences of taking the wrong path.

Since her GP's last visit on the 26th of August 2022, mum had a fasting blood test along with an ECG, electrocardiogram, a test that records the electrical activity of the heart, including the rate and rhythm). September was a month where things were moving and so on the 28th of September 2022 mum was visited at home by a nurse from Avalon House, the visit was conducted by the Dementia team. The nurse concluded my dear mum had Dementia. On Tuesday 4th October 2022, there will be a case meeting between the Dementia team and a consultant at Avalon House. The meeting was to discuss treatment, and for my mother to undertake a brain scan. By updating my brothers regarding mum's decline in her health I would feel so much better by having offloaded my concerns, it had taken a load from off my shoulders. Regarding mum I did seem to take things personally because in my eyes I thought I could make her feel comfortable and for her to live in a secure place, I should not have taken things too personally but it was life at the time and mental health was a new experience for me and I did not fully understand the effect it had on someone suffering with mental health issues.

It was at this stage I felt the NHS system had by now recognised mum was suffering from the consequences of Dementia, it helped to take some of the strain away I was also hoping things would move forward a little quicker.

The Dementia team would then report their findings to MIND Andover, who are the main department who give other NHS agencies a bit of a push to assist a carer to the mental care to help support a patient. The GP surgery would be informed of the results and the way forward regarding mum's diagnosis, it was the Avalon Dementia team and MIND, who would coordinate after mum's diagnosis. During the two-plus hours of evaluation, mum did not know too much of what was going on around her. The nurse was very thorough and at the same time she explained everything in detail to mum. At one point she asked me if I had power of attorney in place, I confirmed I had the Living Power of Attorney, LPA, in place.

Trapped

We continued with mum's booster COVID jabs program, as mum was susceptible to catching covid and it was a no-brainer, once again mum said if she had been living on her own she would not have bothered to have the booster jabs, it was again yet another reason for her to stay with me and once again everyone within the family knew it was the best thing for mum. Having someone from the family keeping an eye on her and of course that someone was me who was keeping somewhat of tight a reign on her to ensure her safety.

The conservatory where she was sleeping, was off from the living room and it was perfect only because mum had easy access to the bathroom which is situated on the ground floor of the house, I had recently tiled the conservatory, floor and to be honest it was a god send, more so when having to clean up and to mop up after any accidents. Also, the floor was flat and level and assisted mum with her mobility issues, of course she was by now shuffling her feet having a flat even floor to walk on was beneficial. Eventually, I purchased a new wardrobe for mum's new clothes. At one stage before we left her bungalow and we had packed lots of her clothes after a time I would have to purchase new clothes for her only because I noticed most of the clothes she packed were threadbare I could tell she hadn't purchased any new clothes for herself possibly for several years, slowly I replaced her old clothes for the new clothes. At one time I purchased a pack of T-shirts for the warmer weather, I took the T-shirts out of the wrappers, and I laid them on top of her bed inside the conservatory. She then popped into her bedroom and she returned and sat on the settee and I could see there was something on her mind, I spoke first "mum are you ok" " She replied, "no that woman is in my room and has dumped some of her clothes on top of my bed, where is she Keith, where have you hidden her"? It took me a while to reassure her and explain there was no one else inside the house I went on to explain the T-shirts were a present from me. I thought at the time poor mum, what must have been going on in her mind, it must have been very frightening for her. It was obvious that Dementia/Alzheimer's was by now progressing at a much faster pace the effects were by now becoming so much worse.

At times I would apologise to my brothers for sounding defensive regarding the advice they would give to me. I may have seemed negative regarding mums care, I suppose it was because I was at the coal face and dealing with many of her care needs, at the time we were talking about what was best for mum, including placing her into a care home, I knew if I did so it would kill her. Yes, it would have also meant I would have my life back it would have taken the stress of caring for her from off my shoulders, I just could not do it to her. I decided to look after mum at home. There was one train of thought at the time if her mind were destroyed by the dementia, she would not know any difference where she was living. At the time I asked my brothers Michael and Garry to give me some space, as I would appreciate it. Of course, they understood what I was trying to say. At this point I just needed some time away from my part-time job, the college had a scheme where employees could purchase extra days of leave. I needed the extra leave so I would be available for the social services visits also whenever the district nurses visited mum. At the time it was what I had wanted to do, mum came first.

The college working year/leave year started on the 1st of August 22. At the time I used up all my leave entitlement it was why I purchased the extra leave up until the 1st of August. I was also open to all the help/assistance from anyone within the family I

asked them to bear in mind not to push me too quickly, as at the time I just needed time to assess everything happening all around me it was such a crazy time. I was juggling lots of balls in the air.
When I spoke to my brother Michael, I agreed with him, he explained whenever mum and dad argued, mum would antagonise him and would try to goad him into an argument. Now it was happening to me. I am a laid-back person and at the same time I am afraid to say I, verbally, fought back and sadly it made mum even worse. At this stage when dealing with her dementia it was a huge learning curve. I explained to my brothers there was something I wanted to let them know. It was a subject that happened throughout my childhood it was mum who always used me as a shield whenever she got herself into an argument with dad. When dad was dying, he told me if he could turn back the clock, he would have stopped mum using me as a shield. I told him it was OK, as it did me no harm, it did frustrate me. I also know it frustrated dad as well.

During the time mum was staying with me, I contacted Swindon Council, regarding mum's bungalow. Someone from the Swindon council, housing department had contacted me because someone who lived locally had reported, to the council and had pointed out mum's bungalow was empty and no one seemed to be living in the bungalow and they thought it was standing empty, the people who had contacted the council mentioned one of their sons wanted to move into the bungalow. I updated the council regarding mum's current situation, and I must be honest at the time they were more than happy, with the situation, but of course, they also wanted me to keep them updated regarding mum's long-term occupancy. So, it was yet another thing to juggle, as I looked after mum.

Trapped

One morning I came downstairs, to find mum had somehow managed to get herself out of bed; and she was sitting on the couch I could tell she was slightly agitated. I greeted her with "good morning mum" she did not reply. I made breakfast along with a cup of tea I then switched on the TV, she then sat in total silence. I enquired with her to see if she was all right, she went off on one of her argumentative moods at the same time, she seemed to turn on me and for no apparent reason. I then left the living room and walked into the garden shed, I just needed to get out of her way and to be honest, her moods were by now affecting me later the same day I informed the mental health nurse of mum's mood swings.

One thing that was obvious to me and it was on occasions, mum's mood swings, could be very exhausting and draining. I was lucky enough to be able to catch up on my sleep during the day. Whenever I spoke to my brothers, to update them on the state of mum's health, after talking to them, mum would accuse me of telling tales. Her doctor visited her on the 26th of August 22 – Where mum accused me of interfering in her life and once again telling tales. Before her GP's visit, I wrote to him hoping his visit and the subsequent examination of mum, would enable me along with the rest of the family to have some answers. All related to the obvious rapid decline in her mental health and of course her state of mind. It was a horrible process to see mum's decline was sadly happening right in front of my eyes and it is a cruel form of torture.

In the same year, I received a phone call from the dementia team in Winchester it was the nurse who last saw mum at the house, and she had called to inform me she was putting mum forward for a CT scan to help to ascertain the type of dementia mum was

Trapped

suffering with. To also see just how much damage had been done to her brain cells. Eventually, mum's CT scan appointment came through for the 6th of December 2022. I spoke to my brothers and I updated them on the latest news, my brother Michael was based in Dubai and as such he could not make it to be with mum during the CT scan, my brother Garry wanted to be there when she underwent the scan. Once again I drip fed the day of her scan I would remind her daily because at this stage she could not remember what had happened the day before, but for some reason, as I repeated the news to her daily, she kind of remembered something, but alas it hadn't sunk in. Garry duly turned up on the 6th and he and I and of course mum duly turned up at the hospital department where the CT scan was to be carried out, it was an early evening appointment. Mum got herself ready for the scan, the scanner operator informed me and Garry of the fact only one of us could be present with mum during the scan process, I told Garry he could go in with mum. I remained outside and sat and waited for mum and Garry to come out of the room after the scan. Once the scan was finished mum left the room and she was very happy I asked her how the scan went, she replied "it didn't hurt" Garry told me the scan results would be forwarded to the consultant at the dementia team. At last, the scan had been taken and now it was a waiting game. If mum had not needed the cataract operations and on top of things and added to the delay was due to the COVID lockdowns. She may have had a CT scan, but that is life, it sometimes gets in the way.

It was a few weeks later I received a phone call and it was the same dementia nurse who previously visited mum she informed me the dementia consultant had by now received the results of mum's CT scan and both she along with the dementia consultant would like to visit mum and myself at home, so we arranged for a

Trapped

date and time. I drip fed mum the news and explained to her a nurse along with a consultant would be visiting the house they wanted to talk to her regarding the results of her recent scan. Mum said to me "they won't put me in a nut house will they"? I reassured her no one was going to put her anywhere she was going to stay with me. I could see she was scared I reassured her, the best I could, she said: "you will be with me when they visit won't you"? I replied, "of course I will mum".

Over the following days, I reminded her about the upcoming visit, so when the day finally arrived, she would hopefully not be nervous. On the morning of the visit mum became agitated and was beginning to lose her temper with me. She accused me of telling lies and tales to strangers, she said I had told people she was mentally unfit, and she could no longer look after herself. The day soon arrived just before the nurse went through to the living room, I heard mum chatting away, the consultant spoke to me inside the kitchen where she explained to me the results of the recent scan it was not very good news, because she confirmed with me, my mum was suffering with both Vascular Dementia and Alzheimer's, a double whammy, poor mum, I asked her if she could mention in conservation with mum she could no longer live on her own, I know it may sound like a cop out but I thought if anyone who found themselves in my position they would have done the same having heard it from someone else and more so someone who worked within the NHS and someone in authority, never the less, never in a million years would I have guessed mum had both Vascular Dementia and Alzheimer's, all I wanted to do was to place my arms around her and smother her in love. I and the consultant then walked into the living room mum could tell by my face something was wrong, she asked me "Keith what is it, it's about me isn't it"? The consultant gently explained to mum what had been found on the CT scan and of course, mum only had to hear the word dementia and the word was like a red rag to a bull, she said: "what are you trying to say to me, are you telling me I am a nutter because if you are, they are not going to lock me away, is that what you are saying to me, I have to tell you I am not mad"? The consultant went on to explain as best she could to mum, she was diplomatic and explained to mum she was unwell and then went on to explain that both the vascular dementia and Alzheimer's were at an advanced stage. I asked if there was any medication mum could take to ease or slow down the symptoms, the consultant explained alas in my mum's case she was reluctant to prescribe medication, due to the advanced stage of both diseases and medication may even cause even more issues such as her vital organs or may speed up the deterioration of mums overall health. I knew full well she was suffering, and it was obvious to me, but I was not expecting mum to be diagnosed with both Vascular Dementia and Alzheimer's, it was a double whammy. Mum was sitting on the settee and obviously looked very worried and I am sure she did not know what was being said to her as she said to me "can I have a cup of tea please Keith"? she asked the nurse along with the consultant if they would like a cup of tea, they declined the offer and said their goodbyes, I walked them to the garden where the consultant informed me she had often seen the same reaction to such dreadful news many times before. She informed me the results of mum's scan would be sent to her GP, and a copy would be sent to me, she also mentioned a Living Power of Attorney, LPA as she strongly recommended, I got them in place before it became too late.

The nurse left me some mental health leaflets to read and it was as I was reading a leaflet I then came across an article which explained in far more detail the ins and outs regarding a Living

Trapped

Power of Attorney, LPA I decided to talk to mum about taking out the LPA's and I was somewhat naive regarding the need for an LPA and I did not go ahead with the LPA's until she was ready to do so. It was over breakfast one morning when she came out of the blue with "OK Keith I will sign those documents now, I have thought about it, and I think it is a sensible thing to do". After she said those words I did not want to think that my lovely mum would or was going to suffer with the results of dementia, I know it may have sounded a little stupid of me, but at the time I just wanted my mother back with me and to somehow get back the person who was her normal batty self and not a shell of her former self. Regarding taking out the LPA's I had to approach mum with a delicate touch, I always explained things in full to mum, even though at times she did not fully understand what was going on around her. The LPA's can be completed online via the government's web page, I thought at the time it would be much better to have a solicitor to complete the forms and to witness the LPA's. Eventually, a solicitor visited the house and before any paperwork was signed, she had a long chat with mum asked her a lot of very pertinent questions and I soon realised what the solicitor was doing by asking the questions, it was to ensure mum knew exactly what she was about to sign. The legal documents would then be signed by the solicitor who would have to state mum had not been coerced in any way to sign the documents, the solicitor informed me if she ever thought my mum was seriously affected because of the dementia she would not and would not have been able to sign the LPA documentation. There are two types of a Living Power of Attorney, LPA, they are Property and Financial Affairs and Health and Welfare. People do not have to choose both as they can select just one LPA, but I felt it would be better to go for both. I am so glad I did only because after the solicitor completed and had signed both documents, she then sent them to the Government agency which would then authorise the LPAs. Over a few my mum's health had deteriorated I do not think a solicitor would have signed off the LPAs because of the state of mum's mind at the start of 2023. A while later the government department sent me the authorised copies of the LPA and I have to say at the time I thought it would not be any requirement to use the LPA alas subsequent events would prove me so wrong.

The matter of help regarding benefits for mum never entered my mind and I had no idea she was in fact entitled to attendance allowance in my case the carers allowance. I can only think it may have been because I did not have experience of the world of benefits, I believe there are some people who could quote the rules regarding claiming benefits also for some people it as second nature for them to apply for benefits.

There were other health issues which at the time were affecting my mum also one of the issues was her blood circulation, for instance, the skin on her legs was as thin as tissue paper it would rip so easily, the first time I had noticed was when I was rubbing some skin cream into her legs one of my fingernails touched her skin and I am afraid to say my fingernail ripped a line of skin away from her leg, I could not believe what I had done, I immediately cleaned her leg and dressed it. I could not apologise enough to mum and at the same time I was upset at having hurt her, it was unintentional. She told me it was OK as she had not felt a thing.

At the same time her mobility was becoming more restrictive her GP fully understood mum's restrictions and luckily, he would visit the house to carry out comprehensive health checks, The first time he visited the house mum said to him "you're from up north? Aren't you, he replied "yes I am I am a Yorkshire man" she

Trapped

replied "I am from Liverpool" it is interesting because after his first visit I would not have to drip feed to her whenever he wanted to visit, I found it strange only because any other person who was visiting her I would then have to drip feed whenever they were to visit the house. On one of the doctors' visits, he noticed the dressings I placed on mums legs to cover the various cuts, he removed the dressings once he had checked her skin along with the various cuts more so the cut where I had managed to accidentally rip off the skin on her leg, he informed me because of the blood and mums fluid circulation issues from now on he wanted the District Nurse team to dress her legs. It had nothing to do with how I was dressing her wounds, he just wanted her circulation issues to be closely monitored.

It was during one of the District Nurse visits when I was asked if I had claimed the Attendance Allowance benefit on behalf of mum, I replied at this point I had not. A day or so later I was talking to my brother Garry along with Faye they enquired if I was receiving any benefits to help look after mum and once again the attendance allowance was mentioned I explained the reason why I hadn't yet submitted a claim for carers allowance, my response to the carers allowance was "no" only because I did not think I was entitled to it. After talking to Garry and Fay I subsequently applied for both allowances and during the process for the attendance allowance I had to attach the dementia consultant diagnosis document and at the same time, I also applied for the carers allowance. The dates I was claiming were from the date when mum was suffering from dementia, and I had made the decision she could no longer live on her own. It wasn't long before I received a letter in the post from the Department for Work and Pensions, DWP, informing me my application for carers allowance had been rejected and seemingly out of hand, I was not entitled to the allowance, the letter stated I had three months to challenge the decision at the same time mums condition was worsening and to be honest I had far bigger issues to deal with such as the everyday requirements of looking after mum. In the end, I forgot about the claim. Sometime later I was talking to my brothers Michael and Garry and it was then I explained about the DWP's rejection letter they both asked if I could send them a copy of my application including the rejection letter and in both of their opinions the DWP letter had made no sense, the letter was not in plain English, it rambled on. A month or so later I challenged the DWP's reason for rejecting my application for the carers allowance and I wanted the DWP to explain to me in plain English why my recent application had been rejected. Also during this period nothing was heard regarding mum's attendance allowance and a couple of weeks later I received a phone call from someone working for the DWP who requested me to immediately re-submit my application for the carer allowance and to wait for an hour for a call back from the same person, I applied online and to be honest, it wasn't very long after submitting the application form, the same caller once again contacted me and confirmed the receipt of the application. I asked what next and he informed me to wait until the DWP had once again contacted me. A week later I received a letter from the department confirming the payment of the carer allowance but it was only for three months only because, in June of the same year, I would be receiving another benefit and it was my state pension once I had received the pension and then the carers allowance would cease to be paid. Only because the state pension is seen as a benefit. It was not very long after the contact from the DWP mum also received a letter confirming the receipt of the Attendance Allowance benefit, but it was to back dated to January

and the date from the issue of the dementia consultant confirmation of Vascular Dementia and Alzheimer's's diagnosis.
The main thing was at the end of the day mum was eventually granted an attendance allowance but during the previous eighteen months I spent thousands of pounds looking after mum and providing the best for her, I did not want her to do without. Alas, the state was very slow, and it was a long-drawn-out process to eventually get the benefit due to her. My advice to anyone on the same journey please try to obtain a dementia/Alzheimer's diagnosis as soon as possible, I realise at the time it is the last thing anyone wishes to think about. Once you have a diagnosis the quicker you can apply for at least the attendance allowance and believe me you will need it, anyone who thinks they can use their hard-earned savings will soon find any savings would soon dwindle and fast. Bearing in mind if you receive a carer's allowance and as soon as anyone receives the state pension the carer allowance then ceases.

I may have previously mentioned I arranged for my mother's medical records to be transferred from her surgery in Swindon to my surgery. It was somewhat selfish, as it meant we would no longer need to travel to mums surgery and as such it helped to ease the burden placed upon me, besides by now it was difficult, to get mum to sit inside my car, to travel for almost three hours and to travel to her village and then return to Winchester. To then spend an hour picking up her prescription and visiting her bungalow to read any mail and for mum to then a chat with her neighbours and those who knew mum her chats could last for a very long time. On a bad day if there were road works, or a road traffic accident, or if there was inclement weather it would take even longer to travel home. Besides, with mum's medical condition and her incontinence, it was not viable anymore.

Trapped

A big drawback to visiting mum's village it was becoming somewhat of a magnet as the bungalow was pulling her back to her village of course it was understandable. I would often talk to my brothers regarding mums bungalow and it was becoming a major issue, one which needed to be sorted and very soon, as it was me who was looking after mum daily I knew full well it would break her heart more so if in her eyes I had blatantly gone behind her back, to hand the bungalow to the council. By now mum and I had a nice routine in place, and I knew what she liked along with her quirky needs. At the same time, she continued to pay rent, council tax, fuel, and light bills along with the telephone bills. It was imperative at this point we somehow handed her bungalow back to the council, as there was no longer any requirement for her to live there, her health by now had reduced her to a shell of her former self.

My brothers and I suggested it was time to somehow get mum to agree for her to hand back her bungalow to Swindon council it was easier said than done. At the same time, it was the most obvious thing to have done as everyone around her knew she was by now incapable of living on her own, as the Vascular Dementia and the Alzheimer's were becoming much worse. I am sure her doctor along with the social services would have had something to say if I took her back to the bungalow and to live on her own. It did not take very long for me to realise my own life was from now on was intrinsically entwined with mum's journey along with her descent into a mental health abyss, from where my poor mum would never return. It did not take the brains of an archbishop to realise I would from now on have to put my life on hold, for however long it would be at the time I did not have a clue. I had committed to caring for mum for however long it would take, please do not get me wrong it was a hard thing to

have done, my brothers and my family kept me sane during both mum's and my own journey together, more so when I was struggling and there was one thing I did know and it was how mum was feeling, trapped inside her mind and was by now slowly being destroyed. It would prove to be a very long commitment caring for mum.
Prior to her diagnosis along with the lockdowns, we would travel into Winchester, and she would go shopping sometimes we would visit a nice tea shop. Where she enjoyed a pot of tea and of course a piece of cake. She was well known as "tin throat" only because she would drink a boiling hot cup of tea and would rarely leave the cup of tea to cool down and would drink the cup of tea piping hot.
During the same time her health was declining I noticed she was losing a lot of her teeth, once again she would not allow me to contact a dentist or to inform her GP, mind you, by now she had lost most of her teeth. Each small health sign was adding up to a far bigger health issue, aside from dementia and Alzheimer's. Everyone in the family knew she would never admit to ever being ill or if she did have any worries regarding her health. That was apart from where money was involved as she would immediately go on the defensive. She may have had a rough upbringing and a lack of education, as a child her family was dirt poor, in later life she was as sharp as a needle whenever it came to figures and more so whenever it came to money. Everyone within the immediate family knew of the background of my mum's early start in life.

At the time I did not need to think twice regarding looking after mum, as she was our mum who gave birth and life to myself and my brothers Michael and Garry, it was her who cared for all three of us boys as we grew up, so it was my turn to care for her in later life, I have to say it was some journey. At times she certainly pushed me to the very limits of endurance of course, towards the end of her life, she was in such a distressed state and her health was rapidly going downhill. During the lockdowns mum and I had a lot to keep both of us occupied, I believe mum and I, at this time enjoyed each other's company. Also, at the time the front garden was overgrown all due to several large trees growing in my next-door neighbour's garden. Mum and I spent many weeks clearing away the Ivy and the overgrowth. Mum always enjoyed mowing the lawn and as such she was put in charge of mowing the grass, she was happy and was in her element, she was outdoors in the fresh air and doing what she liked to do. Besides, she was less chatty which meant I had some peace and not for very long though. One of her quotes was "a person could die of thirst around here", it was a gentle nudge only because she wanted a nice cup of tea. It was also during the lockdowns I would often hear mum repeating herself and she would forget what time of day it was or in fact what day it was. As time went by she was aware I was becoming more and more concerned about her declining health whenever I enquired about her health she would on occasion cease to tell me how she was feeling only because in her mind she thought I was telling tales to the doctors and of course my brothers. At times it felt as though it was a form of emotional blackmail only because one of her responses to my concerns about her was to say, "I am packing my bags in the morning I want you to take me home". Over the years it became her go-to response whenever she became frustrated or, as I thought, whenever she became scared, of what was happening to her, or she could not explain what was happening to her, at the same time, I knew there was something wrong with her, but on the other hand I did not know just how ill she was.

Trapped

So it was we eventually enjoyed each other's company, I am not saying everything was perfect, far from it, it just took some time only because she was inflexible and I suppose she had her own life and she knew most of the people within her village, also since my dad's passing she once again became fiercely independent. Whilst she stayed with me all I ever wanted to do was to look after her and to tell her she would be alright and for her to enjoy life whilst she was living with me I just wanted to treat her as though she was on holiday and to forget about any worries. As I have often mentioned she was well known as a sun goddess and as such her skin over the years had turned into a mahogany colour. It was one of the only vices she had it was hard for her to change her ways. It was her sunbathing which would cause a problem in the future. Her mobility was becoming noticeably limited and more so after she had broken her femur. At times I would help her to finish a sentence she would tell me it was OK and say, "Keith please just forget what I was saying". It was during this time I noticed bruising appearing on her arms and legs, I would enquire if she had fallen over. She would often respond with a firm "no please just leave me alone and stop fussing".

Long before her illness, mum would drink a piping hot cup of tea, and at the time, as I have mentioned she was very well known for having a tin throat, so she would knock back her cups of piping hot tea. Towards the end of her life, she would often forget to drink the cups of tea and would complain the cups of tea were far too cold to drink. Towards the end of her life, there was one cold drink she enjoyed drinking, and it was a nice cold glass of cloudy lemonade. It was hard for me to watch my lovely and eccentric mum become so much worse as the weeks went by, I wanted her to relax and let me care for her.

Trapped

I have mentioned previously whenever mum was staying with me, I had noticed many of her clothes were threadbare and were old. Over time I purchased new clothes and were the kind of clothes she liked to wear such as blouses and skirts also when she could wear them, trousers. Many a time she would say to me "Keith someone has stolen my clothes and have left their clothes; I think someone has burgled the house". The longer time passed she was also finding it difficult to stand up to walk, her balance was going as such it was a very difficult thing for me to witness. Due to her shuffling her slippers would be soaked with water and at the time I did not realise what she was doing, until one day she told me her feet were very sore and I took her socks off and I could see between her toes the skin was red raw some areas were bleeding, I treated her toes and feet soon the skin had healed. I found out the source was because she was walking outside and getting her slippers wet and hence, she was wearing wet slippers and socks, it was yet another thing I had to keep a very close eye on. Mum did not realise the implications of what she was doing. After this episode and during our routines I would check her feet daily and cut her toenails whenever they needed clipping. Mum had plenty of slippers whenever I thought her slippers were either worn or were becoming too dirty, to wear, I would order new ones online and when they arrived I would let her open the packaging and her eyes would light up, especially when she saw them, she always liked the M&S slippers they were her favourites. Talking about her slippers leads me to the time it was a bit of a mystery it was the issue of her dressing gowns and more to the point the mystery of the missing belts, no matter how many times or how careful I was washing her dressing gowns, the belts would either go missing or they got mixed up and would often end up with different coloured belts. It was a detective mystery and one we both enjoyed solving, inevitably I would find the belts under the pillows inside her bed or mixed up with the towels in the bathroom. This brings me to yet another issue, along with her dementia and as I have once again mentioned and it was when she became incontinent, of course, she was very embarrassed and I would try my very best to reassure her it was OK as it was between the pair of us and no one would know. It was lucky my son Paul had helped me to put mum's double bed inside the conservatory, luckily the floor was fully tiled was easy to clean with a mop. My poor mum inevitably would have an accident and during the nighttime she would call out for me to come and help her. I would then rush downstairs only to find she was soaked and her nightclothes would be saturated, thank god I had a washing machine and a tumble dryer, over the last few years the weather has changed and we seem to have more rain than sun, so a tumble dryer is a must when looking after someone who is incontinent. She soon got used to the routine and whenever she had an accident, I would quickly get her out of her soaking wet night clothes and get her washed and changed into her incontinent pants and get her dressed into some clean nightclothes. Then help get her into the living room switch on the television and make her a cup of tea and of course a nice piece of cake. While she sat back nice and clean with of course a nice cup of tea I would quickly strip her bed and then shove the bedding along with her night clothes into the washing machine. I would mop the tiled floor inside the conservatory and wash down the bathroom then place fresh bedding onto her bed. And only then I would sit down to have a nice cup of tea. We would chat away and try to sort out the world, she would always tell me she felt so embarrassed I would try to tell her it was OK as everything could be washed. Towards the end of her life she was by now used to our routine. My sister-in-law Faye advised me to swap out the normal tea bags and switch mum over to having decaffeinated tea bags. Which I did and of course mum could not tell the difference. The reason for switching was that cutting out the caffeine and switching to decaffeinated tea and coffee would improve her bladder health and it would also help to reduce her need to go to the toilet. By reducing the sudden urge to pass urine, it can also help reduce the risk of having a fall which often happens when someone is rushing to reach the toilet in time. Anything to help reduce any falls and help reduce the risk of urinary issues. She became distressed at the situation she had by now found herself in and with only her son to assist her and to help with the type of things she would have normally been able to do for herself. I tried my hardest to reassure her and make her feel comfortable with the situation she sadly found herself in. I have to say if I were in her position I would feel the same way. All I ever wanted to do was to help her and to make her life as comfortable as possible. My mum was a very proud person, and she would keep herself to herself she never wanted to be a burden on anyone including her own family. God only knows what would have happened if she remained at her bungalow, I know the authorities i.e. social services would never have allowed it to happen. We were often offered carers to come into the house to help me look after mum and of course whenever I discussed the option with her and without fail she would point-blank refuse, those who knew my mum would understand why she refused the offers of help, but I have to say at times I needed some help. I would never do anything that would upset mum and I knew full well if I agreed to the offer of help, she would not cooperate and it would have been embarrassing for those visiting the house to help her and as such it was far better to carry on as I had been doing. Also at this point, I did not need yet more stress in my life. I knew I had added to the burden of looking after her on my own. There were many points during the time I was caring for mum when I felt the

Trapped

needed to offload my troubles onto my brothers, it allowed me to offload the stress, sometimes I would speak to my children, explaining how I was feeling at the time. It helped me from going mad, I found, in my case, when looking after someone who is suffering from Vascular Dementia and or Alzheimer's the carer soon becomes a prisoner within the house and at the same time I knew mum was trapped within her mind and she could not just step away from what was happening to her. A carer's previous social life very soon becomes non-existent, and friends slowly disappear. The carer's life becomes solely evolved around the person they are caring for, because looking after someone is always on their mind from the time they go to bed and whenever they wake up. I am ashamed to say my life became somewhat of a sad existence. At the same time, I never once resented mum, every day I could see the huge struggle mum was going through. I know this might seem selfish at the time I knew one day I would eventually get my old life back.

Chapter 5 – The Inevitable

I have a large shed within the garden before Mum's decline in her health, I would "pop" inside the shed to write books and to research the family history. It was a good place to unwind and escape from the crazy world around me. But even that was hard to do whenever mum stayed with me. Often whenever I disappeared into the shed to write a book, I would hear mum crying, as she was sunbathing outside just off the side of the kitchen. Whenever I heard her cry I would immediately rush outside of the shed to investigate why she was crying and on checking on her she would answer through tears "I did not know where you were, I thought you abandoned me and I was so scared". I would then place my arms around her to give her a peck on the cheek and make her a cup of tea if it was a scorching summer day I would bring her an ice cream. It would not be the first time she would cry for no apparent reason I soon became guilty about going into the shed. It may come across as selfish as my life was becoming very restrictive. There was one thing I did like to do, and it was to order goods online whenever the delivery driver arrived. It was only then I would have some form of human contact and of course, it was someone else albeit for only a brief period. I think back to before mum became ill and it was a long before she needed me to care for her, before looking after mum my life seemed very "ordinary" but compared to what my life was like during the time I was looking after mum, I would crave to have my "ordinary" life back once again. As mum's health seriously deteriorated, she began to wake up between 4 am and 5 am and would not know where she was and would shout "Oh god please help me" or "Keith where are you, please help me". As I have previously mentioned, I had my bedroom windows open, along with the bedroom and living room doors were always left wide open so I could hear whenever she needed me, I was woken many times by now I had lost count. Over time I got to know words and sentences whenever she was in pain or if she became distressed. At the same time and over a lengthy period, my sleep pattern was by now shot to pieces. After mum passed away it took me a long time to break away from the broken sleep pattern, even now long after mum has sadly passed away, my sleep pattern is not the best but at least I am slowly getting there. At times I had felt as though I was on my chin strap and managed to get mum into some kind of routine and it seemed to work. The routine seemed to make her feel settled and less stressed. For instance, at times when she woke at 3 am as mentioned the routine was to make sure she got herself washed and dressed along with clean night clothes and fresh bedding, the routine was working and at times she became less aggressive and of course, we would watch the news and to sit on the couch to have a nice cup of tea of course to have a slice of countryside cakes. For some bizarre reason, the cakes calmed her and of course a nice cup of tea. Sometimes once she had drank the tea and ate the cake, I could then gently persuade her to go back to bed of course, other times we would stay up until the sunlight appeared and then our routine would once again kick in and she would get washed and changed into her everyday clothes. As I did not want to keep her in her nightclothes all day she deserved to have a change of clothes each day.

Towards the end mum wasn't eating very much and of course I informed her GP he advised me to give her whatever she wanted to eat and it did not need to be breakfast cereal, etc., he confirmed any food would do to ensure she was taking on board fluids and to keep a diary of what she was eating and drinking. For breakfast, I would give her a piece of dry toast cut into four squares. She never liked butter or spread on her toast and so I would slip in a slice of Ryvita and her cup of tea. If she did not eat her breakfast I would once again give her cake, just to make sure she ate something and of course I was extremely worried about mum, it was killing me deep inside, to see her health rapidly decline. No one could tell me how long she could keep this up, health-wise. I am very lucky to live in a beautiful part of the country and over the years mum enjoyed visiting me and she looked forward to the various walks into the countryside and of course shopping in Winchester also walking around the city, she was not the cultural type of person, but saying that she did enjoy visiting Winchester Cathedral. As her health slipped away, I knew I was losing my mum to such a horrendous disease, that is dementia. Along with her downward spiral, the walks and the visits to the cathedral soon stopped.

As usual Mum was in denial regarding her illness and at the same time my dad had a similar attitude to his health. For me, it was difficult only because I had no idea if she was in pain or not. The only thing I could do was to make her as comfortable and happy as I possible could and whenever I helped her or wanted to care for her, she would always think there was a catch as to why I was doing it. Do not get me wrong. I am sure she knew full well I loved her too bits I just wanted to help her. Along the journey we had our many ups and downs. At the same time, I would contact my brothers to ask them for help and guidance regarding our mum's changing conditions there was something creeping in more and it was the verbal outbursts. I have to say she was never violent towards me.

Trapped

What did become interesting was the fact we developed a kind of sign language, more so if she could not remember a sentence and before she would become so frustrated she would indicate with her hands, what it was she wanted and if I got things wrong or said the wrong thing she would nod, or move her head up and down for yes, and move her head from left to right for a no. So, I would have to understand what she wanted even though it was through limited speech and head movements.

Whenever I thought it was safe enough to work within the garden she would sit inside the conservatory and we would use our sign language and if mum needed to be taken to the toilet she would wave her hands in the air and if she wanted a cup of tea she would wave her right hand, funny enough if she was happy she would wave both hands, at chest level, to let me know she was feeling happy it seemed to work a treat. Often, I would see her with her head in her hands and it would be obvious to me there was something wrong and I would rush to see what was going on. On many occasions, she would cry in her hands with tears rolling down her face. It was such a sad sight, to see mum so upset, sometimes she had no idea why she was crying, and it was something I rarely saw when she was fit and healthy, my dear mum. Whenever I rushed to see what was wrong it was such a sad thing to see, and I would comfort her and would try to find out why she was so upset, and I would try to find out what had triggered such a reaction. Sometimes she would tell me she did not know why it was she was upset other times she thought I had left her on her own and gone into town. At times when she was upset, and I would have to leave what I was doing to take her indoors and sit her on the couch to try to reassure her everything was fine and for her not to worry. I would do what I had always done, and it was to switch on the TV and to select a film, a romantic comedy film, along with a cup of tea and of course a slice of cake. If I did not have a cup of tea with her, she would enquire "Aren't you having a cup of tea with me, Keith"? I would then make myself a cup of tea to reassure her and to show her I wasn't going to leave her on her own so I would sit with her drinking my cup of tea and to have a chat with her, it seemed to calm her I also believe it made her feel safe. It was because of Mum's anxiety and having experienced a few episodes of her becoming worked up, I soon realised being able to leave the house and to just "pop" out had all of a sudden and overnight had been severely restricted I was by now limited to what I could do, such as the things I previously took for granted had by now been extinguished.

The only time mum was OK with me leaving the house and funny enough it was on a Wednesday morning, and always at 6 am to travel to a supermarket as it was only a ten-minute drive, I have no idea why it was. She was always fine with me going shopping at 6 am and for me it was somewhat of a mystery to me. The only downside was sometimes she would lock me out of the house, it would take a while to try and coax her to unlock the door, it was a minor thing but in the greater picture, it showed me my mum's health was becoming a lot worse. The other mystery was after I had been to the supermarket she would say and without fail, I could go for a pint at the local pub on a Wednesday afternoon, of course, I would take up the offer and have a couple of pints of beer it allowed me to chat with others such as the locals at the bar, and of course the bar staff. I would then come home from the pub and of course mum was fine about the whole thing and whenever I returned home, she was never upset. There were sometimes when I did not go to the pub because if she was "off colour" I would stay at home with her. Whenever I returned

Trapped

home be it from the supermarket or the local pub she would always say "Oh I am glad you are back, because I am dying for a cup of tea, but only when you are ready", meaning get the kettle on and fast, it was mum all over.

In the end a Wednesday became something of a routine and often both of us would laugh about the back door and of course mum having locked me out of the house. At times she still had a dry sense of humour, along with her sharp tongue. It would not be very long before I lost my mum along with her sharp tongue along and her sense of humour. My thought process during the time of looking after my mum was to ensure she was as comfortable as I could, of course, it was not an easy thing to do, more so when she pushed against everything, I was trying to do for her. My mum was just like a wild animal trapped inside a cage and the situation she found herself in was doing her head in, more so mentally as she wanted to be able to go outside for a walk alas physically, she was by now incapable of walking.

A very noticeable thing happened to her and once again I have previously mentioned, and it was that mum was by now repeating words and sentences and whenever she was in mid-sentence she would forget what she was about to say. Because of her frustration, she would then fly off the handle and would raise her voice and say "Look Keith I am not going mad and I am not a mental case so don't you dare go telling tales about me to your brothers and I also don't want you telling the doctor" of course I would inform my brothers and would continue to send a weekly list of mums changes to her doctor. I look back on this time like this. I think at the time my poor mum must have been petrified. The verbal abuse was becoming the norm as I have previously mentioned she was never physically violent towards me.

Trapped

It was obvious to me she was succumbing and was consumed by the effects of vascular dementia and Alzheimer's. Mum must have been trying her hardest not to tell me about how worried she was and how she was feeling but at the same time she did not have a clue as to what was happening to her, nor what her mind was doing to her. Who knows what horrible damage was being done to her mind?

When my mum was well she was a very good eater and she had a healthy appetite, but as she succumbed to dementia and to make sure she ate well I would eat my food with her most of the time I would eat the same food as mum, I did this because if she could see I wasn't eating the same food as she was eating and if not she would have refused to eat what I had cooked for her. There were some meals where I did not eat the same food such as breakfast, because for many years she only ate a slice of dry toast along with a piece of Ryveta, it was never an issue at breakfast time. Along with her breakfast, I would get her to take her medication, I would sit with her whenever she took the medication to make sure she had taken it. I purchased a container with compartments and they were marked with the days of the week, I also purchased small plastic cups each cup was a bright colour and whenever I gave her the medication, she would check for what day it was as each medicine compartment had a day of the week printed on them, whenever she had a cup of water to help wash the tablets down she always made sure I gave her one of the brightly coloured cups. I noticed she would seem to forget it was time to take her medication, hence why would I sit with her while she took her medication?

Once when one of the district nurses visited the house, she mentioned what she had called a "dementia" clock, the clocks have a large face and have the day, morning or afternoon & evening, time am & pm also the date is brightly displayed on the clock face. It worked a treat for mum and at various times of the day I would ask her to tell me what was displayed on the clock's face. She did not always get the date or time right, but there again it gave her something to check each day, and it was yet another routine. Towards the end of her life and in her mind, every day was set firmly on a Thursday.

Getting back to her food intake and as mentioned for breakfast she did not eat much and for lunch as she only ever wanted cupa soups, so I would place some biscuits and a packet of her favourite crisps with some fruit on a small plate along with a cup of tea. The evening meal was always varied, I served it with vegetables. Then followed by a chocolate pudding and she enjoyed the puddings I always felt better whenever she ate her dinner.

At one point I thought I would be clever by cooking curries and stews in a slow cooker. But and it is a big but, for instance, on a Sunday evening I would serve her a stew, good so far, but then on the following Monday night I would try to serve her some more of the stew or the curry and she would often say "oh no Keith, I had stew on Sunday night and as you well know I do like a different meal each night" I would reply "bloody hell mum this isn't a hotel you know". Jokingly she would reply "No but it is my hotel" Oh how we laughed, mum was always hard faced. She took no prisoners or fools our mum, gran & great gran was a large character, full of life she is sorely missed.

At the time, my mum would tell me to go halves on the food bill and at the time I was always reluctant to do so, as I thought, Mum

Trapped

being so ill, it was up to me to pay for the food along with household items. It was the way I was, but things changed when I had to give up my part-time job. During this time, I did not wish to allow mum to go halves on any of the food bills and this would make her cross, and she would ask to see the shopping receipts. She did not wish to see the itemised items on the receipt, she just wanted to see the final figure along with the amount I paid. Of course, at times I told her I must have left the bill in the boot of the car, or I had not picked up the receipt. She was adamant she must pay something towards her "keep" as she called it. For me, it was not a natural thing to do that is to take money from my sick mother. I realise for some people it may seem strange but at the time I felt embarrassed and ashamed to ask her to pay for her so-called "keep".

As Mum's vascular dementia and Alzheimer's progressively got worse, I was advised to look at the Legal Power of Attorney, LPA, for both Health and Finance. At the time she still had her mental faculties and long before taking out the LPA's I would talk to her regarding the reasoning for taking out the LPA's. At the time she fully understood what was meant but at the same time she was not happy, only because she thought if she agreed to the LPA, she did not want anyone to think in her own words she was "mad or crazy". After our initial discussions, we left things as they were. Perhaps I/we should have gone about things regarding the LPA differently. People must realise my mindset at the time was in a kind of state of denial, I was also wishing against hope that my mum was not suffering from any form of dementia. At the same time, she was still recovering from the post operation on her femur and was becoming frustrated with herself. You see in the past she recovered quickly from previous injuries, of course her cataract operations. But in this case, the broken femur was

Trapped

frustrating her because she knew how much of a burden the break she was as could not walk on the leg, for obvious reasons.

On the odd occasion, I would give in and would succumb to her frequent requests also her constant badgering to allow her to go outside and to let her attempt to walk to the Littleton Stud, I would try to get her to walk with a Zimmer frame because she had refused to use a walking stick, as mentioned previously she was a very determined and somewhat of a bloody-minded person. As she struggled to walk, we would walk 200-300 metres and we would have to stop at the Running Horse pub, of course, she had done extremely well to get to this point, but I have to say she soon realised she could not walk any further. When we walked home I knew she had taken on far too much and of course, mum was so frustrated with herself only because by now she knew what her physical limitations were, I felt sorry for her as she loved being able to go for a walk in the fresh air. The walk home took twice as long, and my poor mum was by now all in. I had offered to help get her and for her to use the frame, but as always, she was determined to walk home under her own steam. As soon as we entered the house, she was by now exhausted and as always, she said: "Ah that's better, I could do with a nice cup of tea". She popped into the bathroom at this time she still was able to sort herself out, on her own. Problems only occurred if she was wearing trousers more so during the chilly winter months because if she wore trousers the leg had recently been operated on, it would cause her some issues I would then have to assist her. I found apart from the cold winter months I would persuade Mum to wear skirts as it was far easier for her to change herself and go to the bathroom, I was soon learning it was easier for me to help and assist her make things easier for both of us.

Trapped

During mums later months during her illness I would reassure her things would be alright, at the time I was lying to her as I did not wish for her to think about the end of life situations, we would both know when that particular point was on the horizon, as it would be blatantly obvious to everyone caring for her. As mentioned during this time I was concentrating on making her life as comfortable as I could and surround her with love and of course kindness.

Sleep was a huge issue for me because whenever mum woke during the early hours and most of the time she would not go back to bed, during the day whenever I knew she was happily watching a film of course drinking cups of tea, I would let her know I needed to go to bed to try and catch up on some badly needed sleep, as I did so I would leave the living room door and my bedroom door open, it was so I could hear when she would shout out for me. Most of the time I would catch up with an hour's sleep before mum would cry out for me to help her, I would then rush downstairs only to find mum crying her heart out. It was always the same reason, and it was because she had thought I had abandoned her. When she saw me, she would calm down, and I would then put my arms around her to give her a peck on the cheek. I soon came to realise my life had suddenly changed overnight. But on the other hand, and of course it goes without saying my dear mum's life had changed forever and my inconvenience was nothing compared to what she was now suffering. I always knew one day I would get my "life" back, sadly I knew it would be long after her sad demise. Even so "getting" my life back would not be as easy as I first thought.

Previously I mentioned the Living Power of Attorney, LPA, documents I have to say, I had no regrets in paying for the documents to be completed along with a solicitor present. I have to be honest at the time I did not ever think I would ever need to use them or have to prove I had the LPA's, towards the end of mum's life I was constantly having to produce the Health LPA and also when mum passed away I was asked several times to prove I had a financial LPA. The documents had made life so much easier for both mum and of course I. I strongly recommend anyone going through a similar situation with a loved one to get the LPAs in place long before a loved one's mental health deteriorates. I realise at the time it was something a family may not wish to contemplate, but alas a loved one's health inevitably goes downhill the LPA's will be needed. There is a government web page whereby anyone can complete the form, and I had opted for a solicitor to complete mum's forms as a form of belt and braces exercise, it was a personal choice.

I must point out Mum's independence and her forthright stance on life permeates throughout the family from myself and my brothers, along with her nine grandchildren and five great-grandchildren. Towards the end of her life, she could only just remember her sons' names and at other times she could not remember any of us. I must point out my brothers and I had a great and memorable childhood. My dad sadly passed away in 2004 and at the time he was extremely ill having suffered in the past from heart attacks and strokes, there is one thing regarding his death, and he was lucky he did not go through what mum was going through. My mum was dad's carer, I know the experience affected her greatly. I do know if dad was still alive, he would not have wanted her to have suffered from Vascular Dementia and Alzheimer's.

As mentioned during mum's declining health I would keep her GP updated regarding any changes in her health towards the end of her life I would send a weekly update to her doctor. Increasingly I was alerting her GP of her food and fluid intake along with blood pressure readings, her blood pressure was on the low side. At the same time, I was informing my brothers of my concerns and once again mum would often accuse me of telling tales and she would often use the emotional blackmail leverage. I look back on this time and think it would have been so easy for me to have left things as they were, and it would have been so easy. But I am afraid sometimes I did the opposite and I would stand up to mum's outbursts, in some people's eyes it was so wrong of me, at the time all I wanted to do was to care for her and to get some kind of response or for a spark to ignite within her mind, I wanted the mother I previously knew to come back to me. Any kind of response would have been comforting to me but alas I am afraid to say the spark had long ago been extinguished sadly for good, it had left me devasted at the time I realised I had lost my mum for good. I seemed to have gone into a state of mourning for her, knowing she would never again be the same person. I knew I had lost my hard-faced, cheeky independent, and strong-willed mum. By writing the story of mum's struggle with Dementia I hope it will help others going through a comparable situation. You are never alone as there are people along with various agencies that are available, but you will need to find them and must plug in with the agency's assistance. I am going to be political, and it is regarding the social care provision within the UK, no matter what political party is in power, they all pay lip service to adult social care. The situation needs to rapidly change as there are so many unpaid carers in the UK who look after loved ones, and they are not paid, and some are living in poverty by not being paid as a carer. At the same time, they do help save the government of the day an absolute fortune. I honestly believe if it were not for family and in some cases, friends caring for the elderly, the NHS (system) would eventually grind to a halt. I believe most MPs should hold their heads in shame at what is happening behind the scenes. Also, how the elderly in this country are treated. It is also the same for families with children who are sadly going through a very similar situation.

What I am about to write may seem blunt, but I do think it needs to be pointed out. If someone in the family gives up work looking after a loved one who is suspected of having dementia, I must reiterate, at this stage, it is a must to have a loved one diagnosed as quickly as possible because the process might take some time. Initially contact a GP along with your concerns try your very best to have a loved one booked for an appointment with the local memory team and attend a cognitive test i.e. a memory test, if it is then found they have failed the test a CT scan needs to be carried out as soon as possible, if it is then confirmed a loved one does have dementia, it is time to contact the Department of Works and Pensions, DWP. If your loved one does have dementia the DWP will need to see the Dementia consultant's notification documentation confirming they are suffering from dementia. You will then need to apply for Attendance Allowance and before applying check the DWP web page, if you are the sole carer you can also apply for carers allowance, only after the DWP have confirmed the family is entitled to payments and have already authorised the Attendance Allowance. If the sole carer is not in receipt of a state pension the carer allowance will be authorised, but it will cease as soon as the carer has reached the state pension age. The DWP counts the state pension as a benefit and as such you are not entitled to both benefits. In my case mum hadn't been diagnosed with Dementia as it was due to many factors, I was still working part-time whilst initially caring for my mum, I hate to think how much I and many others have saved the

Trapped

NHS in costs, including a bed space, at the same time I did not wish to be a burden on the state. I have to say when I needed help from the state, it was found to be lacking. What I am trying to say is if anyone is in a similar position, please swallow your pride and check at an early stage as to what benefits you are legally entitled to.

Getting back to the everyday care of my mum, I have to say the district nurses who often visited mum and without fail provided excellent and professional clinical care. At times mum suffered from UTIs along with various infections in her lungs more so the left lung. The following is not criticism of anyone within the medical profession. During her final years, mum's surgery prescribed antibiotics because she kept suffering from UTIs and urinary Tract Infections, which is normal for elderly people and seemingly it also goes hand with people suffering from dementia. After a while, I knew straight away whenever she was suffering from a UTI surprisingly it was whenever she had a dramatic change in her moods and would then become verbally aggressive and as I have mentioned previously, she was never violent towards me. I got to know whenever she had changes in her behavior and whenever it happened, I would then contact the surgery, her GP would ask for a sample and normally on the very same day, he would prescribe the antibiotics. It was things like this had made me think about if she was still living on her own, she would not realise what was happening to her or she would not spot the signs something was going wrong and god only knows what would have happened to her, it does not bear thinking about. Linking in with the many UTI's and at the time she was also suffering from pneumonia. As she approached the end of life the antibiotics were struggling to clear the pneumonia.

Trapped

I mentioned previously I knew the best thing I and my brothers did was to get mum out of her bungalow. At the same time, it was the last thing she wanted to happen alas by now she was struggling to know where she was, such as everyday things in life. Of course, I sympathise with the situation. I felt so sad, and I could see she was slipping deeper under the dementia veil. If she was living on her own there would be no doubt in my mind she would have been moved into a care home, against her wishes.

Of course, none of my fears or what was happening to Mum resonated with her there is something I do not think many people may realise regarding someone who is suffering from the effects of dementia. That is, It isn't only the person who is suffering from the effects of dementia and it may seem self-indulgent or even selfish but at the same time my health was suffering, sometimes I would have to put off booking a doctor's appointment for myself, only because mum would have a fall inside the house or she was far too ill more than often we would end up in A&E. Also, whenever she was discharged from hospital, I would spend a lot of time caring for her. So, it was my life that had suddenly become secondary and by now mum was becoming extremely frail, weaker, and of course, her body was slowly shutting down. It is not a moan I am trying to highlight what life is like, and to highlight the reality of looking after someone who is suffering from dementia, and yes I could have placed her in a care home, but I knew if I had she would not have lasted very long in a care home and I knew she would have given up on life.
Slowly by now, she had no inclination as to what was happening around her. I kept what I was struggling with, away from the family and of course my children, yes they all knew what was happening to their gran and it was my decision not to get them involved with the daily care of mum, As I wanted them to

Trapped

remember their gran as the cheeky funny person she was. I was going to care for her no matter what happens, even though it almost broke me.

In 2023 Mum broke her wrist at the time I was in the kitchen, and I heard a loud thud and groaning coming from inside the living room, by the time I entered the room mum was by now sitting on the couch holding her right wrist. I automatically knew something was seriously wrong and at first mum would not let me look at her wrist, I then sat next to her and spoke to her calmly and I gently took a look at her wrist and noticed on the underside of her wrist I could see there was a small lump and there was no bruising, I asked her to try to move the wrist and when she tried she was wincing from the pain. I knew straight away she may have broken her wrist or may have fractured it. I wrapped her up in as many layers of clothing along with a jacket only because it was wintertime and I did not want her to get cold, more so if we had to wait in A@E. I only just managed to get her into my car as you can imagine it was not the easiest of things to have done, because by now she normally could not get into the car, in this case, it was an emergency. It was only a ten-minute drive to the hospital and as I drove the car she kept asking me if I could stay with her of course I said I would be with her during the whole time she was in A&E, I knew why she wanted reassurance, it was because when she broke her femur I was not able to be with her in A&E and all because of the COVID-19 restrictions. Before we left the house, I had packed a bag with some of her nightclothes and slippers also a photocopy of the LPA for Health in case I needed to produce it.

We were not in A&E for very long and mum was being processed, and she was soon seen by a doctor, who quickly got mum's wrist

Trapped

X-rayed and it was confirmed she had broken her wrist. I had by now informed the A&E team regarding her dementia, including the medication she was taking. Mum was wheeled back into a cubicle within the A&E department. The doctor spoke to her and said because of mums current condition i.e. dementia and of course being scared of having once again been admitted into yet another hospital and did not help when I mentioned the word dementia it was then she became extremely agitated and said "Hey who has told you I have got dementia and you are trying to tell me I am mad, Keith come on we are going home" and it took me a while to calm her down, I think if anyone who is caring for someone on a daily basis you get to know the various trigger words and the words which would help to calm a love one. The doctor apologised and asked Mum to sign a consent form and of course, she had refused to sign. Then I produced the LPA for Health. The doctor took the LPA and read it and soon another doctor arrived and he informed me he did not recommend an operation on mums wrist because he did not think in her current medical condition she would not survive the aesthetic so the doctors asked if I could sign the consent form, on behalf of mum. The doctors would pull mums wrist back into position. They had injected some powerful painkillers into her arm, the other doctor took hold of her shoulder and between them pulled on mum's wrist. Eventually, the pair had successfully managed to manipulate the wrist back into place and it was soon placed into a plaster cast, a nurse applied the cast onto to mum's wrist, and she then came out with one of her favorite sayings it was "I bet you don't know where I come from do you"? The nurse replied "No sorry I don't Mrs. Hearn" Mum then responded with one word "Liverpool" and she then laughed, because she was proud of where she came from and whenever she informed others of where she was born, a very proud scouser, at the time of having her wrist set in plaster she went on to tell the nurse about having been married to our dad and she went on to tell the nurse all about their travels around the world and having her three boys. To the best of my ability, I gave an account of her fall. I told the A&E staff about mum's recent dementia diagnosis including the consultant's name and of course her GP's details. This would not be the last of her falls or her trips to the Hospital. On the way home she was a little quiet and said, "Oh Keith my wrist is starting to hurt, and it throbs, I responded with "I am not surprised you have had a nasty break". As we traveled home I thought to myself "well mum, you have just broken your wrist and you have just had it manipulated back into place, and you are complaining about is a bit of throbbing, you are very brave" As we entered the house as always she said "I would love a cup of tea" I thought to myself, good old mum. It was not the end of things, because she had broken her right wrist, which was the same wrist she always used as she was right-handed. Meaning I would have to cut up her meals only because by now could not do it herself, regarding drinking I would have to place a straw in her cups it was easy said than done, she made a bit of a meal trying to place the straws into her mouth and I was far more concerned about the hot cups of tea so I would need to hold the hot cup of tea and it was a bit of a scene mum trying to place the straw into her mouth without knocking over the piping hot cup of tea. Mum had such a short attention span, and she would often get herself worked up and she would become so frustrated often she would appologise for being such a burden and for adding yet more work onto my shoulders. I would respond as it was not a problem just as long as she was comfortable. Her wrist having recently been placed in a plaster cast I would have to assist her even more such as washing and changing her clothes, it wasn't easy for both of us only due to the limitations of her wrist, I found it so much easier

Trapped

for her to wear T-shirts so I had ordered new ones online, she liked the bright colours to be honest she liked wearing the T-shirts. I say this only because if she did not like something she would not wear the clothes and at the time it was no good arguing with her.

At the same time, I purchased a couple of fleeces, a size up from what she would normally wear, it was to enable her, along with my help, to pull the right arm over her plaster cast. As you may have gathered mum was not the easiest of people to please, between the pair of us we had managed to get there in the end. Once again, the district nurses would visit the house every Monday. As I have previously mentioned, I was constantly being asked if I required further help with helping and looking after mum once again I had to decline the offers of assistance and for reasons explained previously mentioned and so it was we just about managed on our own, come what may. I found the routines we had in place were the only way of getting mum out of bed, washed and dressed, in mums case having a routine in place seemed to have worked for her and of course, there were lots of what I would call misunderstandings also at times she would forget what we were doing and whenever we were getting her ready to face the day ahead. When she was confused she would then shout at me and my belief at the time was having some sort of routine in place seemed to have registered with her somewhere deep inside of her mind and to be honest was a major help, getting her ready first thing in the morning, if it had not have worked out at the time, I do not know what I would have done. As it helped both of us and whenever the mornings ran smoothly it had meant the remainder of the day would fall nicely into place. On the other hand, if the morning routines were upset

or did not run according to plan the remainder of the day would then become somewhat of a nightmare.
Mum was extremely resilient and whenever someone first clapped eyes on her a tiny and petite lady they would quickly come to the conclusion she was somewhat of a vulnerable person, when in fact she was very strong both physically and mentally sadly it was long before her diagnosis for Dementia, when her mind was as sharp as a pin. She still had all her faculties, and I have to say at times she was sharper than I was.

During the same time I was caring for her I realised I was not only thinking for myself, I was also having to think for my mum, what I mean is, it was as though my brain had two sides to it, one side was for what I was thinking and the other was trying to predict what mum was thinking and it would somehow work out how I would respond or to have to pre plan for the day ahead. My mind was compensating for mum's mind if it makes any sense? It was because Mum and I were close and over the many years since dad had sadly passed away, and of course, she often stayed with me when I got to know her moods, such as the things she liked and disliked. During the demise of her health, my mind was compensating for her forgetfulness, who knows how our brains truly function, I certainly do not.

During mum's battle with dementia, I have to point out even though I had the LPA's in place, more so the Health LPA's and whenever my mum was admitted to the hospital she often tried her level best to answer the many medical questions regarding her health, she often became somewhat confused as to what was being said to her, this is where I would produce a copy of the Health LPA a legal document and it allowed me to represent my mother and to answer any medical questions on her behalf.

Trapped

Without the documents I would not be able to represent my mum or be able to raise any health concerns, more so as the dementia disease was increasingly destroying more of her brain, I know it is not the technical terminology, I do think people will understand what I am trying put across.

As mentioned, mum would never hold back on what she thought regarding many things my gosh how she would let people know how she was feeling. Many a time my brothers Michael and Garry would phone to see how mum was getting on, and mum being mum would at the time get their names mixed up, this wasn't anything to do with her dementia she always got people and more so their names mixed up ever since we were children. On the same point my son, Paul, her grandson, would often visit my home along with my granddaughter Caitlin. As mum's disease was becoming much worse, she would often repeat the same conversation over and over, of course before the disease she would sometimes repeat herself. It was incredibly sad to witness and at the same time, everyone in the family felt sad, at times she would confuse Paul with Michael, Garry, and Keith. Paul and Caitlin knew their gran and great gran was suffering. Paul and Caitlin were worried about Mum's health and how her health was by now rapidly declining.

It was soon time for mum to have the cast on her wrist removed. We duly attended her hospital appointment of course; she had refused to use the Zimmer frame as she wanted to walk instead. It was easier said than done, but surprisingly she managed to walk to the department, but she did need me to support her, I could tell by now she was becoming very tired. As we sat down to wait, it was soon her turn to see the consultant and as mums name was called out I went with her into the consultant's room, The consultant asked her several questions and then she was asked to go to the x-ray department for an x-ray, and mum being mum said to the consultant "can't you take this thing off my arm, I don't need an x-ray" he looked at her and replied "Mrs. Hearn I am the consultant and I have to make sure your wrist has healed and I can't unless I can take a look at an up to date x-ray" I took her to the x-ray department and I have to say she was by now very tired, I fetched a wheelchair and wheeled her into the x-ray department and it was a good job because we did not have very long to wait after the x-ray and we returned to the waiting room and waited for the consultant to once again call mum forward. It took a bit of a wait, as he had other patients to see first, eventually, she was called forward by now the consultant had received her x-ray. He informed both of us a small bone hadn't quite knitted together, not the way he liked, as such mum would have to have another plaster cast placed on her wrist and before it could happen a doctor and a nurse would have to manipulate the bone in her wrist into place, we waited inside the cast room where mum was given a pain killer a doctor along with a nurse duly arrived and they soon set upon mum's wrist and they were able to manipulate the bone back into place. Then the cast team quickly placed a plaster cast onto the wrist. She was asked what colour cast she wanted and of course, she went for a red one. It did not take too long for the cast to set. Once the team was happy with the cast, we were allowed to leave the hospital we quickly left the hospital. On the way home I could see my mum's face and she was frustrated; I told her it had been for the best the cast would not be on for very long. I was thinking during the journey home my mum had been through so much recently and she had put up with so much, she hated hospitals and was brave to have gone through so much pain.

When we got home mum was handed some paperwork to do with a follow-up appointment at the hospital. She handed me the paperwork for me to read to her. Two words somewhat upset me and those words were "unwitnessed fall" I was somewhat concerned at the wording because it seemed to me as though it had been my fault, at first I thought it was an affront as I was doing my very best to look after her and was trying very hard to keep her safe and well. I raised the wording with her GP and I was informed the wording meant, because no one had been around to witness Mum fall, or been able to explain how she fell, i.e. did she have a dizzy spell when she fell, or had she bumped herself when she had fallen or had she fallen over a piece of furniture, as such it was not a reflection on myself, at the time I thought it meant in some way I was negligent.

The day soon came for Mum to have her latest cast removed, the famous red "pot", once again she was required to have an x-ray on the wrist to allow the consultant to ensure the bone in her wrist had knitted together. As soon as the x-ray was taken we waited to be called forward to see the consultant, eventually, she was called forward into his office, and mum asked a nurse if I could join her, but the nurse informed her I could not join her and I had to remain outside, I knew exactly what would happen if I was not with her. It must have only been five minutes later when I was subsequently asked to enter the room to join mum. The consultant asked me to take a seat and apologised for the mix-up regarding having been told I could not join mum during her consultation, he could see on mums electronic records there was a copy of her Health LPA, and he said he thought there was something wrong with mum by her total misunderstanding of what he was trying to say to her. I went on to explain about her dementia diagnosis. The consultant showed both mum and myself her latest x-ray and pointed out a small bone within the wrist had not knitted together he wasn't totally happy with the results he then went on to point out that if mum was healthier he would have operated on the wrist, but all considered, the wrist was the best he could do. His recommendation was for her to have the cast removed so there would not be any further follow-ups. mum spoke, "thank god for that, does it mean I can go home now"? He replied, "Yes, Mrs. Hearn just as soon as the cast has been removed" we said our goodbyes and once again we sat in the waiting room to be called forward to another room where she would have the cast removed. It was not long before she was called forward, it only took 5 minutes to have the "pot" removed and we were off, I have never seen mum move so quickly. She almost ran out of the hospital and halfway along the corridor she became very weak, a wheelchair and I wheeled her out of the hospital towards the car park.

Chapter 6 – The Fighter

During this period mum was going through the wars, regarding her many health issues and over time I could see she was becoming more and more frail, and she had by now developed a stoop and she was constantly shuffling rather than walking and was no longer lifting her feet whenever she walked as she could only manage to shuffle her feet. I never wanted her to feel she was a burden, but there again she thought she was a hindrance to me, it was furthest from the truth. My philosophy was that mum gave birth to me and looked after and cared for me and my brothers and it was now time for me to care for her I could not leave her an aged parent to battle both vascular dementia and Alzheimer's on her own. I could never do that to her, but there again that is me. It was now my turn to look after mum during her hour of need, I knew it wasn't going to be easy and at the time I did not know what I was taking on, I do not think anyone would apart from someone who is a professional carer or someone who works in the care industry. I did not know the complexity of both Vascular Dementia and Alzheimer's. As I watched on as the dementia slowly destroyed her from within it was scary and horrific for both my mum and me at the same time, I just wanted to find someone who could help slow down the disease or stop the effects of the dementia. I suppose I wanted someone to produce a magic wand and to tell me, for my mum to take a magic pill and then everything would be "alright", of course, it was never going to happen and there were many times I felt helpless not being able to help mum. As the disease took hold of, I knew I was losing the bright, lively, feisty, independent, and very sharp-minded lady, who was my dear mum. It is such a devasting disease.

During this time mum was still paying the rent and the bills on her bungalow, it was at this point and because of the deterioration in her health I contacted Royal Mail and had her mail re-directed to my address. By now It was impossible to drive mum to Swindon. Of course, she was registered with my surgery as it was much closer to my house in Winchester. I have to say regarding her bungalow, sometimes I had my head buried in the sand. That is until someone has looked after a loved one who is suffering from dementia, they do not have a clue as to how time-consuming it is to look after someone who is suffering from the disease. At times as a carer, I would do anything to keep the person with dementia calm and to try not to do anything that will upset them, because the carer must try and calm the person you are looking after. It is far easier said than done and it was what would often happen in mum's case. I had so much to cope with daily and the subject of the bungalow was one less trigger to deal with, for now. I deliberately kept the subject on a back burner. I also knew it was bound to crop up in the not-too-distant future.

My brothers advised me to return mum's bungalow to the council, as she would never live there again her money was better kept in her bank account. For me, it was the thought of breaking the news to mum and I had to bear in mind her fragile state of mind, of course was always at the back of my mind. I had never felt that I was ready to tell her she had to give up the bungalow. Some would have done it without telling the person, for me I could not do it to my mum, just like everything in life, things and situations end up forcing your arm. Also, I did not

want anything to affect her health or create a trigger to upset her. And I suppose I did not want them to face the backlash, I
was becoming exhausted I did not want yet another thing to deal with, such as picking up the pieces, at the time I was dealing with so many other issues daily. It was during 2023 that it was obvious mum was by now bending or stooping and as such she was looking smaller and she was becoming so fragile, both mentally and physically.

I have said this many times and I would often point out mums frailty to her GP, I was not a trained mental health nurse or a specialist at the same time I was looking after an 89 mother who had by now been assessed as having Vascular Dementia and Alzheimer's, yes I was fully aware I could have so easily have placed her into a care home, it was not the option I went for. During this period, as mentioned, she was asking me a lot more about the fictitious "woman" and she would ask me "Is that woman still living in your house"? I would enquire "What woman is that then mum, you are the only one who is living in the house", she would reply "You need to call the police because she has left her clothes in my room", I would often think "oh poor mum, what is happening to you sweetheart"? Knowing full well exactly what was happening to her. At the time she must have been in total fear she could not articulate what was going on in her mind. As such we were both frustrated with not each other, it was more the lack of communication or the inability to communicate for the most obvious reasons. Whenever we found ourselves in this particular situation I would place my arms around her and I would kiss her forehead at the same time I would tell her I loved her she would often reply "I love you too Keith", mum wasn't the type of person who would show her emotions. Times were getting worse for both of us in so many ways. I soon realised I was not just her son, instead I was rapidly becoming her full-time and sole carer. At this point I believe I have to explain in more detail regarding the many thoughts going through my head during this time, I feel it is important to try and explain from a carer point of view, I had no compulsion but to care for mum at the time nothing phased me but what did affect me was the lack of sleep and the pure exhaustion, the more the disease gripped her, I it felt as though mum did not need much sleep, whereas my lack of sleep was draining me of energy. There were times when I knew I could not drive because it was too dangerous to drive when I was feeling exhausted.

As children, mum gave myself and my brothers a backbone and a voice of our own and to use it, also to think independently and to stand up for one another. She was at times hard-faced and could be very blunt, she also had a dry sense of humour. Dad was something of a diplomat and had a knack for calming mum. But as she slowly succumbed to the nightmare effects of Dementia, I believed she deserved the best care and of course, I took it upon myself to deliver the care, I did not know what I was taking on or how much it would take out of me. I also had no idea how I was going to provide specialist care, one of my quotes to her GP was, "I have no idea what I am doing, only because I am not a trained medical person, certainly not a mental health practitioner, her GP knew exactly what I was trying to say. When she first stayed with me there was a discussion regarding placing her into a care home, family members were only thinking of me as they knew how much effort it was going to take to look after mum on my own. At one point I talked it over with her regarding moving into a care home, she bluntly informed me if she went into a care home she would give up on life. I did not want that to happen so the thought of placing her into a care home was off the agenda, I also realised at the time she would often use emotional blackmail on me, as she knew the buttons to press, of course inevitably it would work. I was fully aware of never wanting to distress her as she was going through enough as it was, without adding to her distress.

After having been officially diagnosed with both Vascular Dementia and Alzheimer's it helped to open doors to other medical agencies that provide support to individuals suffering from these horrendous diseases and as such, they contacted me. They helped and advised me as to the type of care available to mum, they were well-intentioned. No one knew my mum nor her stubbornness and as such whenever I spoke to her regarding the assistance on offer, she would inform me in no uncertain terms, that she did not want anyone touching her or assisting her such as cleaning and dressing her, i.e. personal care. I had to pass on her wishes to the care teams. During the early stages of her illness, she was able to clean and wash herself but alas as her illness progressed the simple things became more difficult for both of us. During her decline in health, she became increasingly frustrated both with herself and with the trivial things. During her decline in health, I felt for her it was such a sad thing to witness. At this stage it was obvious her mental capacity had taken a turn for the worse, her weight was worrying because she was going through a stage of eating less and less and forgetting she had either eaten or had not, if that makes any sense. As previously mentioned, I would keep her GP updated more so whenever I would notice any changes in her health. Her doctor would often tell me "Because you are the person who is looking after your mum daily, I shall take my lead from whatever you tell me, and I will take on board your concerns". For me at the time it was a relief to know I could contact her doctor directly, most time after sending updates to him, he would then follow up with a phone call and would ask me more in-depth questions regarding mum's health and her rapidly changing conditions. Whenever he thought her condition was something he needed to personally check on he would "pop" over to the house where he would physically check mum over. Most of the time during her last year she was constantly suffering from pneumonia. I have to say the surgery staff were incredibly good I never once had an issue regarding the medical support for mum.

Going back in time to a time that seems now like an age away, I would like to point out something that takes me back to the 1960's I think may have been around about 1963/64, I was playing on a beach in Aden Southern Arabia. My Dad was at the time serving in the Army and he was posted to Aden when the country was fighting a guerrilla war. We as a family moved to be with dad, mum would not have it any other way. On this particular day dad said to me "Keith, I want you to promise me you will look after your mum for me". I do not know if he meant whenever he left the family to be sent "up country, to a place named RADFAN" as a nine-year-old boy, I took it seriously and I suppose I would keep an eye out for mum and of course, later on during her life, I stuck to the promise I had made to my dear dad. I wanted to point out my reasoning for looking after mum until her dying days, of course, it was my unconditional love to look after her, and as such putting my own life on hold.

Going off at a tangent I would like to point out one thing, like it or not, it is imperative to push for a formal diagnosis regarding Dementia as it is needed to claim Attendance Allowance and Carers Allowance more so if someone in the family becomes a long term carer. The Department of Works and Pensions, DWP, will require a formal diagnosis document from a consultant, who is investigating a relative's dementia.

Over the years my parents were private people, and they did not have, what you would call, close friends, of course, they had neighbors, etc. but they kept themselves to themselves. When mum came to stay with me, I tried very hard to get her involved in village life, but alas it was a struggle and as such I never forced her to do anything she did not want to do. During the latter stages of her disease, she did not realise who my dad, Ron, was anymore and it was as though a large part of her memory had by now been erased. During the many years that Mum came to stay with me, before her illness and during the summer and Christmas holidays she would visit Winchester and of course, she would enjoy getting out to go shopping but what did surprise me, was she was not religious person, she always enjoyed visiting Winchester Cathedral and walking around the cathedral to observe the artifacts within. We sometimes went for a short walk along the water meadows. Whenever we visited the city, we would have a nice cup of tea and of course a slice of cake. She thoroughly enjoyed getting out of the house to do what we all take for granted.

I shall change track and return to the lockdown phase of everyone's life. I have mentioned before it was extremely difficult to explain to mum why we could not just hop into the car and then drive over to her bungalow. During a period of relaxed regulations and because she was still registered with her GP in Highworth, it was only later I managed to have her registered at my surgery. She had an appointment to attend the very first phase of the COVID-19 vaccination program, we drove to the Swindon Steam Railway Museum, which was the venue chosen by

Trapped

the Swindon NHS district to have the very first vaccination program. I hadn't driven around this particular area of Swindon before and as such I ended up parking at the rear of the Swindon Railway Station and unbeknown to me I had parked in a private company car park, it did have a ticket machine for parking and so I had naturally assumed it was open to the public, I purchased an all-day ticket and as I have mentioned I believed it was a public car park. I found the only way to get to the front of the Railway Station, to then head towards the museum, was to walk along a footbridge crossing over the railway line. After walking along the bridge, we ended up inside the railway station as we approached the exit, we were stopped by a member of the railway staff who wanted to know why we had used exclusive access to enter the station. Meaning why we had used the footbridge; he went on to inform me we had been observed on CCTV. I quickly explained at the time I did not know about the bridge being exclusive access and I explained about having to attend the COVID vaccination centre at the Steam Railway Museum. Of course, mum being mum suddenly kicked off, I tried my best to calm her, it was then one of the men asked mum to calm down, well it was like holding up a red flag to a raging bull. Luckily, I had once again managed to calm her down. I asked if they could let us come back the same way they agreed and on the way back to let them know how we got on at the vaccination centre, I believe they were interested only because it was the first time this particular phase of the vaccination program had been rolled out. It was another ten-minute walk to the museum, of course when we got to the site, mum was demanding to find a toilet, luckily, I could see a public toilet and off she went, by now I could see the queue was growing. She shot out of the toilet and began to moan about having to queue. Eventually, we got to the front of the vaccination queue, and at the end of the queue there was a nurse and a doctor who were staffing one of the many vaccination bays. The doctor ran through a list of ailments if anyone had or was suffering from any of the ailments, they could not have the vaccination. Low and behold there was one allergy with which mum, who had almost thirty years ago suffered and it was an anaphylactic shock, she had been stung by a wasp and she suddenly gone into shock, the doctor informed mum because she had suffered an anaphylactic shock in the past she could not have the vaccination as he could not take a chance, he went on to explain even though she suffered with a shock almost thirty years ago, there would still be a residue within her system and at the time the vaccination had not yet been tested against such things as anaphylactic shocks and also they did not know her medical history. I thanked the doctor and before mum could open her mouth, I virtually frog-marched her from outside of the building. As we walked towards the railway station, we were both disappointed of course it meant we would have to wait slightly longer to see if there would be a different and safer vaccination for people like mum.

When we entered Swindon railway station just as we entered the station, I spoke to one of the men who had spoken to me earlier the same morning. He recognised me and asked me how mum got on with having had the new COVID vaccination, I went on to explain she could not have the vaccination as it was due to her previously having a negative reaction to a bee sting and as such she suffered from an anaphylactic shock. He was surprised and replied "That was a waste of time then" I went on to ask him if it was still OK for me and mum to walk along the bridge to once again access the car park. He said, "I shall just let the CCTV operator know." I thanked him before we got to the bridge again mum needed to go to the toilet, I am so glad she remembered to go before setting off on the long journey back home. We walked across the bridge and into the car park, I got her strapped into the passenger seat just before we set off I asked if she was OK because she seemed to be out of breath, she confirmed with me all was OK and to drive the car and get back home. We eventually arrived home and of course the first thing she wanted was a cup of tea. I was a bit disappointed with the outcome of the vaccination, if only when I booked the appointment online there should have been some sort of warning regarding anyone who had suffered in the past with an anaphylactic incident, if so not to book an appointment.

During the lockdown periods both mum and I had so much to do. As mentioned, the front garden kept both of us busy. The front garden had been in for many years in constant darkness it was because of my neighbours whose garden had several leylandii trees, the trees blocked out the light in the front of my house. My neighbour always wanted the trees to be taken down and for some reason, our local council had slapped TPOs, Tree Preservation Orders placed on them, as he could not have them taken down without planning approval. One day out in the front garden there was a Southern Electric tree surgeon who was cutting back some of the large branches from the trees, it was because within the village the electricity supply is carried along overhead cables. As such the branches were almost touching the wires and needed to be cut back. After they finished what they had to do, I was amazed at the amount of natural light that was now streaming into the garden. Mum and I soon set about clearing away the Ivy growing on the tree trunks because the Ivy was by now hanging into my front garden and it needed to be thinned out. Mum was in her element at last she had something constructive to do, she did like to help me and felt happy at being able to help me. She had always been a hard worker and enjoyed working outdoors, over the next couple of days we must have filled over thirty bags of garden waste. In the meantime, I ordered lots of bags of compost because the ground we had cleared was bone dry and was dead, I never saw a single worm whenever I turned the soil over. So, I subsequently spent a few days digging in the bags of compost, and of course my helper assisted me. She was just like a machine once she got started and there was no stopping her, only if a cup of tea was made oh and of course a slice of cake. Over the same period, we must have spent a few weeks clearing the overgrown front garden. We enjoyed the demanding work and of course the fresh air. After a few months whenever I dug over the compost, I noticed the first earthworms squirming within the soil. As soon as there are worms within the soil it proves the soil is healthy and alive.

Before mums' diagnosis of dementia and a few years prior having such a devastating diagnosis, whenever she stayed at my house, she had her bedroom and at the time she was still able to walk up and down the stairs. As mentioned previously her nickname for the room was the B&B room. Those were the good times during her recovery from the cataract operations her heath was seemingly fine, and apart from her eyesight, she seemed to be on the mend, we had no idea what was heading our way it was like an out-of-control train hurtling towards mum. At the same time, I have to admit I was not looking for the signs of dementia only because I was blindsided by her deteriorating eyesight and I was not looking for anything else, I suppose at the time I put her falls and other medical issues down to her eyesight I thought if her eyesight was repaired the falling over would go away.

I realise I keep repeating myself during my mum's summer holidays and whenever she stayed with me, she always topped up her suntan. During the hot summers, she would like lots of cups of tea, I would supplement this with glasses of cloudy lemonade, and she soon took a liking to the lemonade. I mention this only because she was not one for drinking cold drinks. At times during the summer months, the sweat would pour from her skin sometimes I did not know how she could spend so much time under the bright sun, and at the same time, it was the only vice she had left.

Those summer days were a far cry from the time when her health began to decline, one sign that got me thinking and knowing something was not at all well with her was the change in her appetite and fluid intake. Looking back over the past few years it must have been the initial stages of dementia and apart from her eyesight something else may have helped to hide or mask the disease, it was mum's feisty character and fighting spirit. Throughout her life, she would push against conformality as I have previously mentioned she was a feisty character and would tell people what was on her mind, no matter who that person was. What was interesting during her struggle against such a horrific disease slowly destroyed her mind and she always knew the buttons to push regarding my emotions towards her, I suppose it was emotional blackmail, and it remained the same up until her death. During her illness caring for her was never easy and many a time I was pushed to the very limits of my endurance of course at the same time I loved mum to bits.

Throughout my life, I owe mum and dad everything. I sometimes think it was a blessing in disguise that Mum had to undergo eye surgery to fix her cataracts and for her to recuperate with me because she remained with me on and off during the COVID-19 lockdowns. It was something of a blessing in disguise as I believe someone was looking out for her from an almighty height. The family realised and God only knows what would have happened to her if I had left on her own. Life changed massively during the lockdowns and our routines changed forever and I continue with some of the changes from that time, such as ordering my weekly shop online I still order online, nothing has changed. After the lockdowns I would "pop" to Tesco's at 6 am on a Wednesday, since my mum's death I hardly go shopping on a Wednesday morning as I only shop online. At the time my mum was amazed that someone could log onto a computer and have the shopping delivered the following day, without having left the house. During the week mum and I would put together a shopping list and I always made sure I added the types of food she liked, and she enjoyed eating.

During the first lockdown, I temporarily registered mum with my surgery, only because at the time no one knew how long the lockdown would last, including the government of the day. It was one reason why I would have the TV on to watch the news and to listen to any changes to the lockdown or further restrictions. It gave mum something to talk about, I was trying to stimulate her mind, and my thinking was if something resonated with her at least there was some sort of a spark. Also, I wanted mum to realise it was not me who was keeping her indoors, luckily, we had somewhat of a large garden to potter around in. At the time I wished that the then Prime Minister could have visited the house to personally explain to my mum why the country was in lockdown, he was lucky he did not have my mum to deal with daily. There was one thing that changed at the time the disease was progressing and one of the more noticeable effects on mum. That was people turning up unexpectedly to visit the house. If I knew someone was going to turn up, I would drip feed the information to mum, and it might take several days to drip fee. The visit, but as I have mentioned if someone turned up unexpectedly, would freak her out and it would take a while for me to calm her down, she would be extremely agitated for a while. She would ask me not to let it happen again. I could not help it if someone turned up unannounced.

Sometimes I would have to leave her on her own to pop out to collect her medication such as the antibiotics she needed to clear up yet another bout of UTIs. Urinary Tract Infections. But trying to get her to take the large tablets three times a day was a feat on its own, she would make such a palaver all due to the size of the tablets and of course, she had great difficulty when trying to swallow them, I would have a cup of tea and a glass of water on hand to help her swallow the tablets. She once argued with me regarding the tablets and she informed me she did not need me watching her taking the medication, she was not a child. Once she swallowed the tablet, she would tell me if I was not making sure she was taking the medication she would not have taken them, she would sometimes spit the tablets out of her mouth and then would try to hide them. Of course, that was exactly why I always made sure she was taking the antibiotics.

I do know something whenever she stayed with me, mum was always happy and felt secure also she was well looked after, but when dementia took hold and it was destroying mums mind, she never once violently lashed out, I heard stories of where other people who were looking after a loved one suffering with dementia. The loved one would sometimes attack them only because their loved one had thought their family members were strangers and were breaking into their home. For me, I believed mum and I enjoyed one another's company I do know despite all the ups and downs, she felt loved and cared for. But as her health deteriorated, I adapted to her changing needs including her unique requirements. It was so much easier to adapt rather than to push against her changing requirements. So many things I previously took for granted, but by now I had to give up. Such as working in the garden going to my garden shed to write my books, or jumping into my car and "popping" into town, yes as I was caring for mum often I would travel to a supermarket at six am in the morning and always on a Wednesday. I did not realise it then, it would be another three years before I could once again be able to visit the town and not have to think about Mum, it was only because she had by now sadly passed away, even now I sometimes feel guilty. Another thing I gave up and was attending the Annual Remembrance parade, by now mum was continuously losing her balance and she was frequently falling over. My thinking was that there would be many years in the future whereby I could attend future Remembrance Parades. Alas I knew even then I would not have too many years left with my dear mum.

Over the years of looking after mum, I learned to contain my emotions, to be strong even though she was succumbing to dementia, in fact inside I was being torn apart, seeing her demise, it was an awful thing to have to witness.
Suddenly she was having more falls and was becoming more unstable on her feet and often I would guide her to the bathroom and help her to get in and out of the conservatory which had been turned into her bedroom. As time went by her legs were covered in sores and so many cuts and recently her skin was oozing fluids, the fluid was breaking through the skin due to circulation issues. Her feet and ankles were becoming discoloured regularly, once again it was because of circulation issues. The skin on her legs

was becoming tissue thin and I would do my level best to tend to the cuts along with the sores on her legs, I would purchase dressings and cream, before the district nurses visited the house to tend mums legs for a year or so I tried my very best to do what I could for her. Between the pair of us, mum, and I, we somehow managed, we just plodded along. It was during this time the small things were becoming more noticeable, mums' overall health, such as her profound forgetfulness and by now she was repeating herself. She was also forgetting who I was, she even at one stage thought I was the person who cooked and washed for her. Whenever I became deeply concerned, I would contact the surgery at the same time I would update my brothers Michael and Garry. Of course, mum would once again accuse me of telling tales and lies about her, behind her back, of course it was because I was extremely concerned about her state of mind.

More and more she would tell me to "get that woman out of the house", or she would tell me a family was living within the same house, of course I knew it was all in her mind, these things would freak her out and would take such an age to calm her down, only because in her mind everything happening to her was all too real. Whilst all of this was going on, mum was not sleeping, by now she was reducing her food and fluid intake, and the decline in her health also her inability to get herself around the house, and the falls added to her hallucinations, by now I was slowly getting out of my depth. Her paranoia was yet another stage in the demise of her health. It was such an awful thing to happen to her, I felt so sorry for her, and it was also upsetting me watching her decline.

During each stage of the demise in her health, all I could do was watch and make notes for her GP, I felt helpless because I was used to being able to do things for her and sort out any issue she had, sadly not now, it was beyond my capacity I had to leave it to others, such as the medical professionals. She was so frightened and very confused regarding what was happening to her. I felt for her, not knowing what was happening. She did not even know she was so ill. During the summer months whenever the sun was high in the sky and tempting everyone to go outside, mum would immediately head outside to sunbathe at the time I would sit her in a horrible kitchen chair without any arms to support her. But after a while, I would find her sprawled on the ground, of course, she had fallen out of the chair. I know this may sound very silly to others, but I soon realised her balance was by now nonexistent and whenever she fell asleep in the chair, she would then fall out of it. Poor mum, whenever she fell out of the chair she would never cry out in pain. I quickly purchased a sun lounger with arms to help keep her safe, but now and then she had managed to fall out of the lounger. So, when outside I would work in the garden where I could keep an eye on her.

There was a particular day when I was writing in my shed, and I could hear mum crying. She was sunbathing as usual; it was the first time I had heard her crying. I grabbed my laptop, and I rushed outside to make sure she had not fallen out of her sun lounger. I still had hold of the laptop close to my chest and I missed a step and went flying. I landed onto the side of the laptop, and I hurt myself. I managed to find mum and she sat upright on the lounger. I could see she had been crying and of course, I asked her if she was OK and she blurted out "Oh god Keith, I thought you had left me all on my own, since you are here could I have a cup of tea". What could I say? Another time I found mum lying on the ground this time she was complaining of pain in her ankles, I felt her ankles and I asked her if it was painful whenever I gently moved them she said she couldn't feel any pain so I then checked around her knees and I could see some swelling and bruising around her knees, whenever I tried to move her knees she winced in pain. She confirmed both of her knees were painful to the touch. I kept her on the ground in case she may have broken or badly twisted her knees, I made her as comfortable as I could and wrapped her up in a quilt because she was lying on the ground. I called the emergency services and explained how I had found her on the ground, I went on to explain about mums' diagnosis of Dementia, and by now she was frequently falling. I was informed a paramedic team would be sent as soon as possible and not to move mum and to keep her nice warm. After a while, mum could not understand what all the fuss was about as she could not remember falling over. She became agitated and became verbally aggressive towards me. Eventually, two paramedics turned up at the house and began to assess Mum, all the time she kept saying to them "Look I do not know why you are here, I haven't hurt myself", one of the paramedics asked her "Mrs. Hearn, how did you end up on the floor"? Mum replied, "I don't know, it's Keith overreacting and telling tales about me again". One of the paramedics was by now sitting in the house typing on a laptop. The one with mum spoke to me and told me as far as he could tell mum seemed to be OK, apart from some serious bruising around her knees, he advised me, in this case, they would not be taking her to A&E, I said: "Oh I am very sorry for calling you out on pretenses". He informed me it was not a waste journey, far from it because I had done the right thing, more so as mum was suffering from Vascular Dementia and Alzheimer's as such falls overtime would become a regular occurrence and would only become worse. The lady updating the laptop said "Mr. Hearn I have updated your mum's records regarding her latest fall, I can see she has had a few falls already. I then became a little concerned and said to her "I hope you don't think I am neglecting my mum because that would be wrong of anyone to suggest", I had been up most of the previous evening with mum and to be honest it was yet another thing on top of everything else. The lady informed me no one thought I was neglecting mum, but someone suffering from Dementia over time their balance goes, and all falls need to be recorded, she also mentioned mums GP had been updating her medical records. With the information I had been sending him every week, the GP also added all his observations regarding mums' health. When the paramedic who was examining mum outside came indoors with mum, it was then I recognized him as one of the paramedics who arrived at the supermarket car park the previous February when she fell over and broke her femur. At first, he did not make a connection, he then said, "Yes I do remember now, you have a good memory, we see thousands of patients, it is a small world isn't it". Before the paramedics left the lady turned to me and said, she had updated Mum's medical records and asked me to speak to mums GP and inform him the paramedics had been called out over the weekend, he would have seen our latest notes and if he wants to contact you he will. The paramedics then left, and mum was extremely relieved because not only had she been on the ground for a few hours waiting for the paramedics but more importantly she was relieved in the knowledge she would not be going to A&E.

It was fast approaching the end of January 2023, and I had decided to leave my part-time job to solely care for mum, we could not carry on the way we had been, something had to give. Because I was initially denied Carers Allowance and I was fighting the DWP for the carers allowance I had taken the decision to cash in a previous company pension "pot" and it was only because that way I was able to carry on looking after mum without having financial problems, I knew full well a large sum of my pension would have to be paid to the taxman. So, in January 2023 after Christmas and New Year, I reluctantly asked the management, at the local college, to let me leave without having to give the mandatory notice. It was agreed I could leave on the 1st of February 2023, and the weight was immediately lifted from off my shoulders, I knew I could not work and care for my mum, her health was on a downward spiral. When I informed her of what I had done, she did not realise she was working, poor mum.

As previously mentioned, I was exhausted caring for mum, but luckily, she adapted to the various routines we had put in place. During the period of looking after her, I felt as though the government including the various government departments had let my dear mum down. Because caring for someone and having given up work to care for a loved one. It is as though the state does not wish to know how someone can care for an aged relative. I initially applied for the various benefits, available, but in our case, we could not apply as mum had not yet been officially diagnosed with Dementia, and as such our initial applications for benefits were thrown out by the DWP, in our hour of need. Thank God I was able to cash in a hard-earned works pension, it allowed both of us to survive, as mentioned it was a private works pension, and it was a pension I was going to use for my retirement. At this point, I had to wait for mums' official diagnosis of Dementia, before I could reapply, for the attendance allowance again. I know this is something any government department would not wish to hear about, it amazes me, how we often hear in the news regarding people who weren't born in this country who seem to be fraudulently claiming millions of pounds in benefits, and yet people who work all their lives paying into the state pension for decades are then rejected when claiming for benefits, it makes me very angry. Mum's GP surgery including the district nurses advised me regarding the various care packages available to help mum. The problem was mum was such a strong-willed character and she would not allow anyone from outside of the family to visit the house or to help. I had some idea of how someone with Dementia their health would eventually deteriorate, I have to say I had no idea of the reality of what would be involved in having to look after mum and more so as she slowly deteriorated in front of my eyes, sadly I was not prepared for it, nor the physical and more so the mental toll on myself. At the time I looked at things this way, mum gave birth to me along with my brothers, and in her unique way, she managed to look after the three of us. It was now my turn to look after her and in her hour of need, as I write this part of the book, I am somewhat upset thinking about how my mum suffered, please do not get me wrong, mum was never the easiest of people to live with and at the same time I did not have to think or weigh up the pros and cons of caring for her, it is what people do.

As I keep mentioning, mum was very well known within the family along with her friends, she was known as being slightly scatty, and she would never hold back on her opinion and never conformed as being a "normal" mum, part of the reason for being the way she was it was all because early on in her life, she had to look after herself and would have to stand up for herself, as her father had passed away when she was a little girl. When she was eventually evacuated from Liverpool to the Chester countryside during the Second World War, she thoroughly enjoyed the Cheshire countryside and was so happy. Looking back on our lives she passed on that self-preservation attitude to all of us, my brothers and myself, it has permuted down the generations. Having said that dad had put up with a hell of a lot, when he was

Trapped

alive, living with mum. I am sure at times he must have been aware of when mum "flew off the handle", I do not mean violently I just mean when her mouth would run away with her, I have so much respect for dad. I know he and I did not always see eye to eye, it was only because we were so similar, we both had Mum's interests at heart. Going back to the days when dad and the family were based in Aden, South Arabia, dad visited the family on one of his R&R, Rest & Recuperation, we were as usual at the local beach. I was a strong swimmer even at the age of nine. I could see dad scanning the seas with his binoculars only because he noticed our mum was no longer on the beach. Michael and Garry were a few years younger than me and dad could swim only for a short distance for some reason he could only swim underwater. I could see Dad was by now talking to himself and as he put the binoculars down he looked at all three of us boys and said "Keith look son you are going to have to swim out and get your mum back, I think she has fallen asleep on the lilo she is now being carried further out to sea. I replied "but I can't see her dad and I don't know where she is" dad then placed the binoculars onto my eyes and moved the lens over my eyes and pointed me in the direction where he had last saw mum, the lens were focused I could see my mum had gone over the "shark" net and was floating out to sea. I dropped the binoculars and ran along the beach into the sea where I then swam like hell towards where I last saw mum, it seemed like ages before I caught up with the lilo, Mum wasn't moving and I shouted at her and quickly realised she was asleep, at the time she did not know what all the fuss was about. I then grabbed the ropes from around the lilo and began to pull her back towards the beach. By now I was swimming against the tide, my arms were aching, and I was struggling to get mum and the lilo to safety. Eventually, I managed to get her back to the beach. She still could not understand what all the fuss was about, and dad then spoke to her in a loud but firm voice. She always knew when dad was annoyed, and it was always whenever she had pushed the boundaries with him.

During May 2023 I reluctantly decided along with my brothers to hand mum's bungalow back to Swindon council. Everyone knew there was no way she could be left to her devices, her state of mind and her physical health were obviously by now too far gone, and she was incapable of caring for herself. Before handing the bungalow back to the council, I spoke to mum about what we were doing, but alas there was no reaction to the news, a few months before the decision to hand back her bungalow, she would have flown off the handle, so for a few weeks after informing her of what we, myself and my brothers were going to do, regarding the property. Mum had by now totally forgotten about the bungalow and she could not remember what had been said. My brother Garry and his wife Faye were not at all surprised as Faye and her family had gone through a similar thing with her parents. Sometimes mum would say to me she wanted to go home, she did not know where home was, of course hearing this I would have to tell her small lies, I hated doing it to her, having to tell her lies, as I had always been honest with her. My poor mum, looking back, was for the best of reasons.
It was at this stage mum finally received the Attendance Allowance and it helped me pay for the various things I needed to support her whilst I was caring for her, it massively helped, as mentioned early in mums story dealing with dementia at early stages, or if someone in the family may suspect a loved one may have the first signs of dementia, push and push, if you truly belief a loved one is suffering with dementia, push for a diagnosis as soon as possible, at the time you may not want to push for a diagnosis, my experience is if you are someone who is caring for

a loved one during the early stages of illness and you do not wish to place a loved one in care and if you are working as the disease progresses there is no way you will be able to care for someone with dementia as the condition will only get worse as time goes by. The DWP will not action an attendance Allowance or a Carers Allowance application without a formal diagnosis for dementia written by a consultant. These can take an exceptionally long time from being referred by a GP to having a cognitive test and the results then being passed onto a consultant and then waiting for an MRI Scan. I was eventually successful in obtaining the carer allowance after it had been initially rejected. The carer allowance was paid for just two months until I reached pensionable age, then it was stopped. I was informed since I was by now in receipt of a benefit which was the state pension. So, at the time, there were two pensioners, one caring for a pensioner and one who was slowly dying from the effects of Vascular Dementia and Alzheimer's at the same time I was paying for her care, using my state pension. My personal opinion is the whole business of adult care in this country is a total disgrace, as I have previously mentioned people pay into the system as soon as they start working until old age when people such as my mum need state support it is no longer there. It beggars' belief how when we hear on the news regarding Organised Criminal Gangs, OCG, who are somehow able to defraud millions of pounds from the system. I kept all this away from my mum as I did not wish to have her worrying about money as she battled for something far greater.

Over time and due to her illness, it became more difficult to communicate with her and more so to understand what it was she was trying to say to me. At times it was obvious she did not know what she wanted, and as such I would have to make her mind up for her. As time went by and the illness was by now rapidly becoming so much worse, she was not the same person, it was incredibly sad to see this happening to her and now daily. Some may say I was too close to her and as such I was overreacting. One thing that did give me strength and it was the fact her GP and the nurses who were looking after mum, never once thought I was overacting. The stage came when she was not taking on much fluid or food, it is yet another stage people go through towards the latter stages of life.

It was at this stage and it was very noticeable she wasn't the same person, by now she was a shell of her former self, I realised I had by now lost her to dementia, this may seem hard and selfish but I knew I had lost my mum. Only because she wasn't eating or taking on board fluids and as such I would treat her and also give her whatever she wanted to eat, yes it may not have been very nutritious but at least she was eating and she was drinking something and as such I was giving her ice cream, cloudy lemonade and whatever else she would eat for tea. The issue was she was not eating much. Her weight was drastically dropping and by now she was looking more like a skeleton, I tried so hard to get her to drink the high-protein drinks but alas she did not like the taste and would spit the drink out as she was struggling with the taste.

I often thought to myself, whenever I looked at her, I would think "God knows what the hell was going on inside of her head" It must have been a living nightmare for her. At times I felt helpless as I knew there was nothing else, I could do for her, nor could the medical agencies, I realised the disease would run its course and the family could only wait for the inevitable end. During the remainder of her life, she would fight against me caring for her, and as mentioned luckily it was only verbal aggression and not physical. Towards the end of her life, she started accusing me of beating her up, and when she first accused me I was shocked as my world collapsed around me, I was mortified, and I immediately informed my brothers and also her GP, as it was a huge change in mums condition. The following day I informed mum of what she had accused me of, she told me she could not remember, and burst out crying, I sat next to her told her it was OK, placed my arms around her, and cuddled her, the deterioration in her condition was obvious to me and I knew she was by now on a downhill spiral.

Everyone within the family is proud of mum, everyone knows her life story and where she was born, a tough area of Liverpool. Meeting and marrying dad were the best things she did. He provided a good life for mum and of course his three boys.
As mum's health deteriorated in front of my very eyes, I often thought it was good idea she would stay at my house during the summer holidays and at Christmas. It meant she was used to living with me and more importantly she knew the layout of the house and it was not a strange place. During the latter stages of her dementia mum would become upset. Normally she was not an emotional person, she would always be in control of her emotions. By now she would become very emotional for no apparent reason, many a time I would find her crying and when I enquired to find out why she was so upset she would often say "Keith I am not going mad, please don't let them take me to the mad house, please promise me you won't lock me away, please promise me", of course I would promise her she was not going anywhere. Mum's words for a care home were, madhouse, or nut house, only because in her mind a care home was another word for a mental institution. I truly believe whenever a nurse, doctor,

or specialist visited the house, mum would think they were visiting and to take her away, of course, it was the furthest away from the truth. She knew if I was by her side she would feel safe. Besides, it had never entered my mind not to be by her side, no matter what.

And so, it was we were heading towards Christmas and New Year 2023 even though it was a difficult year for mum, in a way we were both looking forward to what 2024 had in store for both of us. I wanted mum to enjoy what 2024 would bring. During the winter months, I once again planted hundreds of daffodil and tulip bulbs. During the winter months of 2023 I planted daffodil and tulip bulbs around the garden. I took mum outside to look at the gorgeous flowers, she enjoyed walking around the garden with my assistance and I could tell by the look on her face, she always enjoyed seeing the amazing colours. Over the past few years including the various COVID-19 lockdowns we had Christmas on our own for obvious reasons, whenever my son Paul and granddaughter Caitlin were able to visit the house at Christmas time, mum and I would wait until they both arrived at the house, it was a hard thing for mum to do because she would get excited only because for a few days before Christmas day and under the Christmas tree I would pile up her Christmas presents nicely wrapped, well I say nicely wrapped up, I would do my very best. As soon as Paul and Caitlin arrived mum would then open her presents, she would rip open the wrapping paper, or she would ask me to unwrap her presents, we made such a fuss about her. As I have mentioned, she did not have a nice upbringing and everyone in the family knew as a child she never had a Christmas. Whenever she stayed with me over Christmas, I tried my absolute best to spoil her. I, Paul, and Caitlin would laugh watching mum opening her Christmas presents and then piling up her nice presents next to her, on the couch. There was something she enjoyed, and it was the Christmas tree with the baubles and glitter. She would point at the lights on the Christmas tree, and every night when the tree was up, she would ask me to switch the lights on and to keep them switched on, she once told me the lights made everything look so Christmasy. I look back on this time and I wish I could have the time all over again and be able to have many more Christmas's with her. One thing I do know is she fully enjoyed her Christmas with me along with the family. At this time of year with Christmas dinner and of course the many tubs of sweets, she would hunker down on the couch along with her favorite sweets of course along with a nice cup of tea or hot chocolate. Even though by this time she had lost several teeth she would always insist on eating her favorite hard sweets such as the toffees.

There was an advert on the TV promoting a woman's perfume and whenever mum saw the advert she would sing "Daisy, Daisy Daisy. Over the past couple of years, I have bought perfume for my daughter because it always reminds me of my mum singing "Daisy, Daisy, Daisy. The present had so much meaning to me.
Getting back to the sweets I was amazed at her preferring the hard sweets at the time I thought if it kept her happy it would do her no harm, apart from the one time I had to perform the Heimlich maneuver. Only because she had somehow managed to swallow a whole toffee sweet and managed to get it lodged in her throat. She panicked and I could hear her gagging, her arms were flying all around her, I looked over and I could see her lips had by now turned a blue tinge to them. I grabbed her and then forcefully pulled them from behind and carried out the Heimlich maneuver, luckily the toffee flew out of her throat. I then calmed her, and I gave her cups of water, it took some time to calm her

down. The following morning, she sadly had no memory of what happened the previous day.

Over the years I eventually lost the TV to her and it was all because she was an avid "soaps" addict, to the point during the last year of her life she would get what was fiction and what was real life mixed up and would become very frustrated with me, that is if I did not follow what she was talking about, such as what had recently happened on the TV and what was happening within the house, such as TV characters moving around the house. TV was intruding into her life on the other hand she did not have much to do or could do during the last months of her life, as such I would have the TV on for her and as her health worsened I would have the TV on for most of the day, at the same time I did not just plonk her down in front of the TV and leave her, I would try my very best to talk to her and try to communicate and engage with mum. The issue was of course her incontinence and she would have accidents only because by now she had lost control of her bowels, so it would take a long time to organise her such as changing her clothes washing her, and getting her into clean fresh clothes, and of course the washing had to be dealt with. In the end, it was constant cleaning, washing, and seeing the laundry. But she was never left in soiled clothes. She was often checked by the district nurses; I would leave the room, and they would check for any sores but what I did not know is they were also checking for bed sores and the pooling of blood. They would often comment on just how clean mum was. By now mum's overall health was rapidly declining.

The winter months posed a major problem, whenever the sun was high in the sky, it would become an issue, as mentioned mum was a sun goddess even in the winter months and she thought it

Trapped

was OK to sunbathe, no matter how cold it was outside. At times she would be dressed in just a skirt, T-shirt, and slippers I would catch outside, sunbathing in mid-winter. The sun became a big issue for me, only because mum thought that if the sun was out, it was OK to sunbathe. I would try my very best to persuade her to come indoors and into the warmth. Of course, it would then lead to arguments she would dig her heels in. Only because in her mind whenever the sun was out, she thought it was a nice summer's day, I would eventually get her indoors to get her warmed up quickly. I would at the same time check her feet and her blood circulation, sometimes her hands and feet would be tinged with a light colour of blue, once again it was all about circulation issues, obviously dressing in summer clothing and sunbathing in mid-winter did not help. I would often try to explain to her if anything ever happened to her, i.e., becoming ill due to her sunbathing in the cold winter months, I would have a lot of explaining to do. Some of the things she did would scare me, only because at this time she was very frail and of course, she was not eating or drinking very much.

On many occasions I would sit with mum throughout the night only because she would not sleep or whenever she had an "accident" in bed, I would often catch up on some sleep later the following morning. Once again sometimes when I came downstairs after catching up on an hour or so of sleep, I would walk into the living room only to find mum wasn't around and I could feel a cold draft blowing into the living room from the kitchen, to find the kitchen door wide open and find mum asleep on the garden lounger only wearing a thin jumper, leggings, and slippers without any socks on her feet. It was freezing. I had to gently wake her up. I would then have to try and coax her indoors, without scaring her or making her feel anxious. I told her she was being very silly sunbathing in winter. Of course, there would be trouble, and I would have to face the arguments, she would accuse me of denying her something with which she enjoyed, and as such I was not being fair. Her way of hitting back was to threaten me with taking her home. I knew full well she did not realise the danger she had placed herself in. The following day she would complain of feeling unwell and cold. Towards December of the same year, mum's sleeping routine drastically changed, I would be woken at all hours of the night only to find mum sat upright in her bed and I would find her rocking and shouting at me. This was yet another noticeable change in her ever-changing moods, it was towards the end of her life, and I found her becoming more verbally aggressive towards me. If it was early in the morning, mum and I would clean her and change her nightclothes and bedding and I would try to get her back to sleep. Inside the conservatory, where her bedroom was, there was a nice comfortable chair and I would make both of us a nice cup of tea or a hot chocolate, of course along with a nice piece of cake. I would also sit there talking to her about anything and everything under the sun. We had so many laughs, and I would try my very hardest to get mum to talk about how she was feeling and if there was anything else I could do to make her life more comfortable.

On one occasion, I once again had been up all night with mum, I was exhausted at the same time I was done in, it had been a hard few days, for both myself and of course mum. She was in one of her argumentative modes, please do not get me wrong, the arguments were the toughest part of caring for her, of course, it was one of the side effects of the disease. I lost my patience and asked her to stop arguing and allow me to have some peace, of course since she had moved in with me, I knew I would

Trapped

eventually lose any vesture of peace which I had previously enjoyed. As previously mentioned, I could cope with the washing and cleaning and to also keep her nicely dressed and doing tons of laundry on a constant basis. But the one thing that did push the boundaries and it was the continuous arguing. At this point caring for her was the constant "accidents" At the end of the day we both seemed to manage, or I was able to manage. As she was by now incapable of looking after herself.

It was fast approaching Christmas, and as such I ordered our Christmas food online and it was to arrive on the 23rd of December. I had decorated the house and of course, put the Christmas tree up along with the baubles along with the lights and tinsel. But for mum it did not seem to register it was Christmas also the tree did not seem to register with her. She could not get around the house without the use of a Zimmer frame, it was a sad sight watching her move around. There was another thing I had noticed regarding mum, and it was because she was getting smaller, I realised it was because she was stooping a lot more as this happens with older people. One morning as I helped her to wash and get dressed she informed me she had fallen sometime in the night, once she was dressed I helped her into the living room and immediately checked her over, she informed me her knee hurt and I checked her knees and ankles, one of her knees was slightly swollen there was also some bruising, but she seemed to be OK. At the same time, she suddenly shouted at me "Now I am seeing a different side to you, you drunkard" Her behavior was becoming more bizarre and was so out of character. A few times she would accuse me of being a drunkard and an alcoholic but once again after a nice cup of tea and a piece of her favourite cake, she seemed to calm down.

Trapped

As previously mentioned, whenever there was a change in mum's behaviour, I would inform my brothers and of course her GP. She still was not eating very much, apart from the slices of cake. Sometimes she would think she had already eaten, and she was not feeling very hungry, it would take a while to get her to eat something as if it were all in her mind. Her mood swings were becoming more frequent and once again, I must point out, that she did not have physically violent mood swings, she never once attacked me. During the past year, she became delusional and was prone to hallucinating, if she was hallucinating it normally meant she had a UTC, Urinary Tract Infection and when she was hallucinating I would immediately inform her GP who would on the same day prescribe antibiotics I would sometimes have to drop off a pee sample at the surgery. I am afraid UTIs became a norm for mum and so did the taking of antibiotics. Towards the end of her life sometimes a UTI would clear after taking a course of antibiotics but then sometimes after only 48 hours, she would have yet another UTI. Poor mum, it must have been so terrible and very scary for her.

At the same time, my brother Michael pointed out to me mum was doing remarkably well to get to this stage in her life, considering her upbringing, and of course, during the 2000's she was our dad's full-time carer. By now she was suffering from the effects of both Vascular Dementia and Alzheimer's. Another change in my mum's downhill spiral regarding her health was the fact she did not know the difference between night and day. She was suffering from sundowning. During the evenings I would try my hardest to persuade her to go to bed, most times she would get very angry with me and she would fight against going to bed, so I would stay up with her until she was ready to go to bed, we are talking about getting into bed in the early hours the following morning. Whenever she woke up, I would talk about the arguments and her not wanting to go to bed, and of course, she did not recollect anything about what had happened. As mentioned at the same time I had a part-time job at the time I found that I could no longer continue working as I felt I was taking somewhat of a major risk, so on the 1st of February I left work to be mum's full-time carer. Looking back on the time, I am happy I gave up work because mum's health was by now rapidly going downhill and she could not cope on her own. From a selfish point of view and considering how she was suffering, leaving work meant by now I was cut off from any kind of social life, I had lost contact with friends and I could not visit family, I was lucky my son and granddaughter were close by and would visit the house, at the time it was once a week. For me at the time, it was such a relief to have someone else to talk to, as I have mentioned when caring full-time for someone, your social life is non-existent. The daytime/nighttime scenario often referred to as sundowning. It is a word that describes symptoms that people with dementia including Alzheimer's at a specific time of day, it is usually during the late afternoon or evening. In my mum's case during the latter stages of the disease, it became increasingly early. Sundowning can include agitation, confusion, anxiety, aggression, and disorientation.

There was one time I left mum with my son Paul, as I had wanted to attend the 40th Anniversary of the ending of the Falklands War and there was to be a parade in honour of the many veterans of the war and of course for those who did not return, it was to be held at Blandford Camp, Dorset, both of my brothers Michael and Garry who had served with the Royal Signals during the war. They were both at the parade and Garry had organised it for me to attend. It was wonderful to be able to leave mum with her grandson and for me to watch my brothers during the parade. I was constantly on edge, and I often contacted Paul to make sure mum was not getting out of hand. As soon as the parade was over, I attended a lecture and soon after I shot home. When I got back mum was fine, but it had been somewhat of a revelation for my son. He told me his gran did not seem to know who he was.

I do have to say I was offered a care plan to assist in caring for mum, but I knew she would not like it, she once said to me she did not want her dignity being stripped from her, as she put it "it is bad enough you having to help me, I do not want strangers, people who I do not know helping me" so I had to turn down the offer of help. There was another side to my mum, and it was whenever someone in a position of authority ever visited the house, she became a different person. She always told them whatever it was she felt they had wanted to hear and would tell them everything was just fine, she would say "Keith can cope I just do not know what the problem is", knowing full well she was being selective with the truth. It was another thing I was not happy about and it is with any government, it does not matter what party they belong to. How would the system cope if everyone caring for a loved one, submitted the cost of caring for their family members to the government to pay for the family members' care, the NHS would suddenly be on its knees, and it would no doubt bankrupt the government. Yet the government does not seem to care, they do not place the taxes where the money is desperately needed. I thought of the situation regarding mum when we were at home and with the front door locked, we were on our own, and we never complained as we just got on with it, I believe all governments and MPs should hold their heads in shame the way carers and their families are treated in this country. We are out of sight and out of mind.

Trapped

Whenever anyone from the NHS visits the house, be it a nurse, her GP also anyone from any of the mental health charities. They could immediately see through mum due to their past experiences when visiting people just like mum. It was obvious to me to anyone who came to visit mum to provide medical care that Mum was indeed extremely ill, her frailty was obvious to everyone who saw her at the time, as she walked the shuffling of her feet was becoming more pronounced. At this stage, she was finding it very difficult to get herself up from off the couch even though I had purchased a special cushion for her to sit on and to provide some extra height to enable her to get herself up from off the couch and under her own steam. It proved just how weak she had become. Instead, as time passed, I would need to assist her to get up. As she became weaker I could see the frustration etched on her face and was so becoming angry with herself, bearing in mind she was a lady who was independent and self-determined to be able to do things for herself by now she needed assistance to wash herself and to get up from a chair or the couch.

There was another issue, along with the many other issues, the problem with looking after someone who is suffering from Vascular Dementia and Alzheimer's is the person you might be looking after, may look as though they are fully conversant with all around them, when in fact they become incapable of understanding or may not know what is happening to them or what is being said to them. My mum's biggest issue was by now the fact she could not remember what had gone on the day before and it was as though overnight her mind had been wiped clean and of course the following day we would have to start all over again just as though nothing had ever happened. I continued to explain everything that involved her, and I would continue to involve her in the everyday activities. Many a time as we approached the end of her life she could be confrontational and "bloody-minded" at times the simplest of things such as wanting to watch her favorite TV "soaps", she would get it into her head I was stopping her from watching the TV, it was because sometimes she had forgotten how to switch on the TV. After I switched the TV on and then selected the program with which her "soap" was on and she would thank me, it was heart-wrenching to witness just how her mind was deceiving her. Of course, I did not mind whatever she watched, it was the least I could do for her. I have to be honest I did not have a clue as to what she was going through, I did learn very quickly how the disease was affecting her, it was a massive learning curve, and whenever anyone visited the house be it the dementia team or the district nurses they left a lot of information with me regarding the various stages of dementia or what to expect as mums circulation began to shut down. As previously mentioned mum's eating and drinking fluids habits began to change also the different types of food that she would normally eat had changed, as such I had to change her "menus" and adjust the size of her plates of food, it wasn't long after mums diagnosis of dementia a district nurse recommend I use a red plate when making mums food at the colour red resonates with dementia patients. At this point in my mum's journey, it was very important to monitor how much fluid she was taking onboard, by now her weight was plunging, she was never a large-sized lady she was such a petite person, as she could not afford to lose too much weight.

Throughout her life mum was a fighter right up until she sadly passed away, she became extremely ill and was fighting for her life. As a child, she was a fighter, but I am afraid this was one fight she was going to lose.

Getting back to the rapid decline in her health, the skin on her legs had by now turned to tissue paper and on occasions when I helped to get her dressed, I would accidentally scrape the skin on her lower legs. It was awful to think I had hurt her and added to her woes; At the time I could not forgive myself. The tissue-like effect on her legs was once again due to her poor circulation issue. On the occasions whenever I had accidentally scraped my fingernails along the skin on her legs, I could see the skin peel away in front of my very eyes. I could never apologise to her enough. The wounds on her legs would never heal properly. I always did my best to clean and dress her wounds. Every three months mum was administered the B12 vitamin jab and had her wounds cleaned and dressed by a District Nurse. At one stage a nurse looked at the wounds I previously dressed and after she took the dressings off mum's legs she could see the wounds weren't healing, as such I was asked not to dress the wounds anymore as the district nurses would clean and dress the wounds and would monitor the progress of her wounds, during each visit they would take photographs of mums wounds, as they wanted to ensure she would not have more sores, more so especially her ulcers the photographs would help to compare the pictures to ensure the wounds on her legs were closing up and healing.

Sometime later mum's legs would swell and at the time I noticed the fluid was breaking through the skin when I first noticed the fluid I quickly took some pictures and immediately sent them to her GP, it wasn't too long afterward he then visited mum and when he checked her over he spoke to me and informed me he could tell my mum's heart did not sound right and at the time he called it a medical term and went on to explain it was linked to mums circulation and why her heart wasn't working properly also why the fluid was oozing from her skin. He also said mum's left lung was sounding poorly and he could hear wheezing sounds whenever he listened to her left lung as he checked her back. He informed me he would go back to his office and would text me when a course of antibiotics was ready to collect, the antibiotics would help to kill the bacteria which had alas built up inside her lungs, and he would also notify the District Nurses to come and visit mum as soon as possible to dress her legs and to clean and dress and to monitor the fluid oozing from her skin. The following day a District Nurse arrived and as she checked mum's legs she mentioned, in front of mum, the words Vascular Dementia and Alzheimer's, this time she did not bat an eyelid, normally she would be annoyed at the mention of the disease. At the time I did not think she knew what we were talking about. It was during this visit I asked the nurse if mum was capable of living on her own and looking after herself, she replied she was not in any state to be left on her own. It was at this point mum replied she no longer cared about what was being said to her as she thought she would soon be going "home" Also if she had her way it would be sooner rather than later.

It was in 2023 that my brothers and I agreed to hand back mums' bungalow to Swindon council. By now there was no way she could ever live in the bungalow, certainly not on her own. As always, I spoke to her regarding the handing back of the bungalow, of course, she did not like the idea. At the same time, I spoke to my brothers, Michael, and Garry, regarding what we were going to do, such as sorting out who packed everything within the bungalow and what needed to be thrown away. I contacted the council and at the same time the various utility companies. When I informed mum about the arrangements regarding the bungalow, of course, she was angry with me once again she accused me of going behind her back and telling tales. She also thought I was lying, and I was telling tales behind her back, which was furthest from the truth.

Trapped

By now both my brothers, including my sister-in-law, Faye, were concerned as I still had not asked for help with looking after mum. They knew full well I was unknowingly cutting myself off from everyday life. The life I had previously enjoyed also doing things which would help me to relax when I was looking after mum, relaxation was a word I thought I would never enjoy hearing again. At this time mum's skin colour was very pale and it had a yellow tinge. Also, as time went by, she found it difficult to swallow and as such I would have to cut her food into small manageable pieces. She would often tell me she had lost her appetite, but I would try my absolute best to get her to eat something. I would give her food I knew she would enjoy eating along with chocolate pudding and of course a slice of countryside cake. I would always sit and eat with her and of course, I would try to help her if ever she was struggling to eat.

Towards the end of life, I could hear a rattling sound emanating from within her chest, it was by now very audible. Many health issues were coming to the fore such as her hands and feet being very cold along with a blue tinge to the skin. It was also becoming difficult to understand what she was trying to say, which also made her feel even more frustrated. It was during this period that both of us produced a rudimentary form of sign language, one which both of us could understand, it came in very handy later. Regarding her issues such as being incontinent by now the routine we had in place was much easier nothing was easy for mum but we had an understanding even with her deterioration in her health, something had sunk in and we would work things out, I am not saying it was easy. More so for my mum, poor thing. In the latter stages her hallucinations became stronger and were becoming frequent. One aspect of mum's deterioration of her health was whenever she was sitting upright on the couch or in bed, her eyes would be wide open, but she would be in a vacant state, it was slightly freaky to see. It was things like this that made me feel her condition was rapidly deteriorating. At times she would complain of feeling unwell and she was very scared. I would wrap my arms around her and try to coax out of her what was making her feel so scared. She could not tell me what it was, it made her feel even more scared because all she knew was something was happening to her, but she could not understand exactly what it was. There were so many days I would worry about mum and what it was she was suffering but of course, at this stage, she was unable to tell me what it was.

There were many days I would seriously worry about my mum, it was not like I had never worried about her, it was a natural reaction, while I was watching mum succumb to the devastating disease that is Dementia. One weekend mum did not get out of bed all day as all she wanted to do was to sleep, at the time she was taking strong antibiotics for yet another bout of UTIs, Urinary Tract Infections. I honestly thought she was by now at the end-of-life stage of Dementia, of course, I am not a mental health or medical expert. Of course, I reported the change in her situation to her GP. In the latter stages of mum's life, I was desperately trying to get all the NHS teams to work in unison. I had a strong impression I was becoming the coordinator for all the NHS agencies; I was trying extremely hard to coordinate a response to my mum's deteriorating health condition. Whenever mum slept throughout the night, she would always have an accident in bed. By this stage of caring for her, I had plenty of bedding, of course, her night clothes. The situation took me back to when she would talk to me about her childhood, and only having old coats to sleep under on a rusty old bed frame. There was no way on earth as my mum was succumbing to this dreadful

Trapped

disease which by now was rapidly eating away at her brain, she never going to suffer under my care. As the days passed, she became incredibly frail, and she was by now suffering.
One particular evening mum could not go to sleep after having an accident, so once again we stayed up all night watching the News on the television after having eaten many slices of her favorite cake and of course plenty of cups of tea, it was the only fluid, apart from the odd glass of cloudy lemonade, mum would or could drink. We enjoyed one other's company where she would ask many questions, some of which I could not answer. But later, in the morning mum had a fully blown argument, what was scary was it had come unexpected, by now you would have thought I would have gotten used to it, but I never did. Once again, I would always keep her GP along with the dementia team updated on the changes to her mental health. Towards the end of mum's life, my brothers agreed she should stay with me, only if I was up to it.

On another weekend I had yet another shock, one Saturday morning when I woke mum up, she was extremely confused and was shocked to see me, but as she put it, "I thought you were dead" She then became teary and said "oh Keith thank god you are alive, I am so pleased, I don't know what I would do without you" I said "so am I" she replied "your dad's just popped out to the pub" bearing in mind my dad had passed away in 2004.
One morning mum decided to have an argument with me over my late dad. It was at this point I heeded my brother Garry's advice, to just step away from the arguments, I felt I had to explain unless anyone had been in a similar situation, the confrontation soon became relentless, and at the same time, I was seriously worried about mum's health. I did walk away from the situation and when I came back into the living room with a nice cup of tea, she once again continued the argument.

Chapter 7 – The Writing on the Wall

Alas, the arguments were becoming more frequent and I had once again made contact with my brothers because I wanted to let them both know how I was feeling at the time and it concerned our mum. At the same time, it was good for me to be able to talk. As I had to let off steam who better to do this with than my brothers? I am not writing this story to embarrass my mum's memory far from it. I feel if someone is reading this book they might spot similar signs that Mum was by now showing and long before she was eventually diagnosed with Vascular Dementia and Alzheimer's. If this story highlights similar traits with their loved one and I will have succeeded in what I have set out to do.

So far I was lucky in the fact I did not have to lock doors or hide the keys to the front and back doors, that was until one winter whilst I was asleep and as I was sleeping I could faintly hear someone calling out my name, I woke and checked the alarm clock I could just make out it was only 4 am. I then shot downstairs as I entered the living room and I could see Mum wasn't in her bed then I noticed the kitchen was in pitch darkness but I could feel a cold wind blowing into the dark kitchen I saw the back door was wide open and as my eyes adjusted to the darkness I could just about make out the shape of my mum who was lying on her back inside the side conservatory, I quickly switched on the kitchen light and at this point, mum called out and she was complaining she could not get herself up from off the floor. I was so relieved to find she was able to say something I told her to stay exactly where she was and I then checked to

Trapped

make sure she hadn't broken any bones. I asked her what was she doing outside and in the dark. Once again she told me she wanted to sunbathe. After a while I just about managed to get mum onto her feet and as we walked into the living room, she was confused. I put the heating on and got her a spare quilt and I tried my best to get her warmed up, of course, she was frozen, I did not know how long she had been lying on the cold tiled floor. I could see there was a frost on the ground outside and she was very lucky I had heard her cry out because where she had fallen was just outside of the house and as such it is very difficult to hear someone upstairs especially from my bedroom. She was very scared and of course, she was feeling very vulnerable. From that moment on I had to lock the back door at night and hide the key in a safe place. I could not have mum unlocking the back door and falling over in the cold at all times of the day. Again what was becoming more noticeable was her verbal abuse, as mentioned previously by now she had begun to swear at me this was a major change in her behaviour because during the whole of my life and up until that moment I had never heard my mum swear. My poor mum I was feeling for her it was once again becoming very obvious things were becoming much worse.

At this point, I and my brothers were making the arrangements to hand over her bungalow to the local council. The delay was my fault only because at the time I was becoming overwhelmed by Mum's rapid decline in her health and by her demanding needs and now my life was focused on Mum as mentioned the decline in her health. I once again mentioned the bungalow to her and to be honest I was somewhat surprised at her reply. This time she agreed it was a good idea to get rid of it. But there again I knew by the following day she would have forgotten about the bungalow. It was at this time I could no longer travel from

Trapped

Winchester to Swindon as those days had by now long gone. My mum was becoming too frail and she could no longer walk even with the aid of a Zimmer frame alongside having to take antibiotics for her bouts of pneumonia the virus was returning on a more frequent basis. Mum's mind was definitely playing tricks on her sometimes she would get herself in a right pickle and she would once again argue about my late dad "Ron" who as I have mentioned passed away several years ago. At times I would try my hardest to extract myself from the living room and once accused me of never having met her "Ron" as I was her carer. It was heart-wrenching, to hear what she had said to me. By now she didn't recognise me anymore.

As usual, I informed her GP he decided to visit her to once again examine her. By now he got to know her very well at the same time she would never tell him anything about the state of her health, mind you by now I don't think anything was registering with her anymore. He read my recent updates before he visited the house and had a clearer picture of what was going on with mum. Once again he found an issue with her heart and could hear a crackling sound within her left lung once again he confirmed mum had once again a bout of pneumonia and it always seemed to be within the same lung, the left one. He left the house and confirmed with me as soon as he returned to the surgery he would text me as soon as the antibiotics were ready for collection.

Her GP was well aware of how over the past month Mum's physical and mental health had rapidly deteriorating. The cuts on her legs weren't healing and recently she had an ulcer at the same time her legs were swelling with yet more fluid and was by now oozing from the skin and once again it was put down to her circulation issues, which in turn were linked to her heart. One of the nice District Nurses, who had attended to mum was very worried about her legs, so much so she asked me if I could stop treating her legs and to leave them to the District Nurses, she updated mums medical records, along with her observations regarding mum's skin colour and more so the yellow tinge around the eyes. The Nurse left the house and later the same day Mum's GP made contact with me to say he had recently read the Nurse's latest update to my mum's medical records. He asked me to once again check her eyes to see if her eyes and more so her pupils, to confirm if had turned yellow, I confirmed they weren't too discoloured. He informed me if there were any further changes to let him know as soon as possible. Once again she was suffering from a UTI and was on a different strength of antibiotics. By now the UTIs were becoming much more frequent. She was also becoming confused regarding the everyday things, they were such things perhaps most of us would take for granted. She was also becoming very angry and frustrated of course at the time I could wholly sympathise with her. It was by now deep winter and the temperature was cold it was time for mum to be dressed mum in warmer clothing at all times, I always made sure she was wearing a clean pair of socks along with a clean top and a nice warm jumper or fleece along with a pair of trousers. As time went by it was becoming more difficult to change her incontinence pants especially whenever she wore trousers. Now she was incapable of changing herself and I found it much easier for her and of course, myself to dress her in a skirt along with a pair of socks, if she wore trousers she would only cry through frustration because the trousers were very difficult for her to put on and to take off, even with my assistance. Due to her "accidents" I had to buy many pairs of slippers for her she always had nice dry slippers to wear.

Trapped

The issue with my mum's health and the medical checks by both her GP and the district nurses and having to be admitted to the local hospital became a regular occurrence it was obvious to me and of course my brothers it obvious to us that mum did not have long to go before her body would eventually give up the fight.

By now her health was declining at such a rapid pace her breathing was becoming shallow and the rattling noise deep within her chest had once again come back along with the rattling chest and by now she had a constant cough. It became somewhat difficult to understand what she was trying to say. She was also hallucinating and she would inform me about a woman who was inside the house and was stealing her clothes along with her underwear. Mum was becoming more unsteady on her feet and added to all of this she had informed me she was feeling dizzy. It was at this time she informed me she had already eaten when she hadn't. I immediately informed her GP regarding mum feeling dizzy he asked me if I had a blood pressure monitor, I confirmed I had one and then he asked me to take her blood pressure on the hour until the early afternoon, I sent the blood pressure readings to the surgery after having sent the readings I then had a phone call from her GP he informed me a colleague of his would come and visit mum sometime later the same afternoon. The doctor from the surgery duly arrived she hadn't seen my mum before and of course, mum hadn't seen the doctor either. Mum was examined just like her own GP had done, her blood pressure was still low once again her lungs were struggling with yet another bout of pneumonia. I had a long discussion with the doctor and at the same time, I could tell by her voice that there was something she had wanted to say to me. We discussed palliative care and end-of-life care. This was the first time someone had discussed end-of-life care. The doctor informed me she would be talking to mum's GP regarding palliative and end-of-life care. After the doctor's visit, I sat with mum, I did not wish to tell her what had been discussed, even though I knew mum was by now dying, it was a lot to take in and to hear those words from a doctor. My brothers weren't shocked at the time and I think I was in a state of shock. I put it down to the fact I was with mum every day and I was watching her slowly die. There was one thing I did have trouble with and it was whenever I was looking after her it was the constant arguments and it was somewhat of a nightmare as the arguments wore me down, all I ever wanted to do was to care for her, but I have to say it wasn't the "old" mum only because by now it was a person who was very poorly and had no idea of what she was doing or saying. Another aspect was as her mental health deteriorated she was by now hurtling towards the end of her life there were constant emotional breakdowns and at times she would suddenly burst out crying, for no obvious reason. But alas I never knew what the trigger was and sadly she didn't know herself. In the past, she was never emotional it was unusual and emotional for me to see her in her current and sad state.

The changes in my mum's health were becoming more frequent and of course her change of moods were becoming far worse as time went by. I knew it was down to the disease, Dementia, which was slowly destroying her mind. The knock-on effect was her brain was by now shutting down her body and her vital organs which all affected by the disease. For those who are professionals and look after dementia patients, I suppose this is what could classed as the norm, regarding patients who are suffering from end of life, they would see it all of the time. For me, it was all so new, and it was such a horrible thing to witness

Trapped

my dear mum who was gradually being destroyed from within and watching her struggle.

As I have mentioned I have not written the book to complain I decided to write it to hopefully help others who may find themselves in a similar position. As dementia took over and it was destroying my mum I soon realised she was by now totally "gripped" by this horrible unforgiving disease, she did not deserve to go through this, no one does. At the time I was dedicated to looking after her. At some time I contacted the dementia team and more so the consultant to enquire if there was any medication which could help mum to sleep or to make her feel relaxed at night. I was informed there was a drug called memantine, alas in mum's case, it was not recommended. At the same time, I did not want my mum to be prescribed drugs that may have turned her into somewhat of a Zombie state. By now Mum's health was on a downward spiral over one particular weekend I needed to contact the NHS 111 service. After explaining to the operator about mum's medical background and what was happening to her on this day and the reason why it was I was contacting 111. I informed the operator about how I was by now finding it difficult to arouse from her in her comatose state. The operator took my details and gave me a case number she informed me someone would be in contact with me. Not very long later a Doctor contacted me and concluded mum was suffering from yet another UTI and asked me to contact her GP as soon as possible. I thanked her, mum had to wait another 24 hours to be able to talk to her GP. I wrote an email right there and informed her GP of what was happening to my dear mum. After a few hours, I was able, with a lot of difficulty, to get her out of bed and I tried my best to reassure her that everything would be OK we just had to wait another day. She was by now so frail

Trapped

and she was very confused, if it was a UTI, it was making mum feel and look much worse. The same day she was in a total state of confusion also she could not make any sense of her surroundings. The following working day her GP once again visited mum and this time he came armed with antibiotics. He gave her a thorough checkup and confirmed she once again had a UTI also her blood pressure had once again dropped. He checked her chest and confirmed he could once again hear a rattling sound within the left side of her chest. He told me anyone suffering from Dementia will have a sudden drop in health and they would never improve as they will have plateaued out for a while until the next medical emergency came along.

During the latter part of 2023, I was becoming more and more concerned about mum not taking on board adequate fluids. She was becoming very weak and she began to sleep on the couch during the day. I was watching my dear mum slipping away. She was constantly telling me she did not feel well and it was so sad as I could no longer do anything for her, I felt so helpless. All I could do was to inform the medical staff and her GP of her demise. If she did manage to get to sleep during the nighttime it was a blessing for Mum and I, because at this point, mums health was deteriorating at such a rapid pace, before going to bed she would argue with me regarding having to go to bed, we had a routine where we would try to go to bed around 9 pm and lately she would fight with me and would go to bed @11 pm or 2 am, I am afraid most nights she woke up during the early hours and she would shout out for me and of course, I would need to change the bedding including mums nightclothes and wash her, there was also an added issue, as I have mentioned many times it was her verbal aggressiveness. The following mornings I would get her dressed ready for the day ahead, I would never keep Mum in

night clothes, only because even if she did not know what was happening to her, I thought we needed to differentiate between nighttime and daytime. Whenever I spoke to her regarding the arguments the previous night she would always tell me she didn't have a clue. The other aspect of her illness and it was she was becoming more upset and it was by now a frequent occurrence.
It was during this period I once again informed her GP of the situation mum and I found ourselves in. It was by now grinding me down and I was not getting much sleep I told him about one of the things which was getting me down and it was the constant arguments. I can reflect now as I write the book, for the past three years my life changed exponentially only because by now my social life and of course my daily life were non-existent. One of the things I used to enjoy was to drop everything to travel to the Isle of Wight for instance. On the other hand at the same time I was looking after mum must have been so scared not knowing what was happening to her.

As her situation worsened I was contacted by the surgery trauma team and they discussed with me mum's deteriorating health and they brought up the subject of DNR, Do Not Resuscitate. It was terminology I had heard of before and it was time to decide on DNR bearing in mind Mum's quality of life, at this point she did not have any quality of life and she was only just existing. Regarding DNR rightly or wrongly, at the time my thinking was if she took a major turn for the worse she may have ended up in a vegetable state. I have to say I did not take the decision lightly and the decision would keep me up at night. It did not rest easy for me.

At times I find this hard to say my mum was sometimes a difficult person to live with, I often reflected on how my late dad would frequently have to calm her down. The same year I informed my brothers the Vascular Dementia and Alzheimer's would not necessarily kill mum as it could be one of three things or all three. These would be a stroke, heart attack, or pneumonia. Of course, they knew mum was seriously ill. They also knew I would do my very best to care for her. Also I would also try my very best to make the time she had left with all of us, a loving and caring time.

Once again she had pneumonia and was placed on a course of antibiotics. As always she informed me if she was living on her own she would not have taken the medication, I knew full well it would have been the case and hence why she needed to be with me. More so when I truly believed she hadn't long left.
It was during late 2023 and I informed my brothers I did not and sadly think mum had very long to live, I did not mean she only had days or weeks left, I had a gut feeling, as it was inevitable and at some stage, but it would be soon, it was only a matter of when and not if. After a couple of courses of antibiotics her chest once again seemed to have cleared up. I did not realise someone who is suffering from Vascular Dementia and Alzheimer's would be prone to chest infections and more so pneumonia along with many other dementia-related diseases. After she recovered from this particular bout of pneumonia, she was sleeping much better and was by now sleeping for around ten hours. Her sleeping throughout the night helped me to catch up on my sleep. At the same time, her aggressive behaviour was more subdued also she was much calmer. At the same time, her mental state seemed to have taken a turn for the worse. I noticed she was once again hallucinating and she was becoming somewhat delirious and it was becoming more frequent. By now I needed someone in the medical profession to be open with me and to explain to me what stage mum's illness was at, also just how much more could her

Trapped

body take, I knew she was a very strong person, alas the pneumonia and the various illnesses must have been taking a huge toll on her. I was becoming more and more concerned I was upset to see her succumbing to such a dreadful disease. As previously mentioned mum's GP would often visit the house when he did he would do as much as he could to make her as comfortable as possible, be it the medication for her UTIs or the pneumonia. Her lungs and more so her left lung must have been in a right old state this time her GP prescribed Doxycycline, as soon as she finished the course of antibiotics she seemed to brighten up, and would look a lot better of course, she felt so much better. Alas it would never last very long and the episodes of hallucinating seemed to be much more intense and became confused about her surroundings, it was so sad to witness, my poor mum was by now a lost soul, she was more unsteady on her feet. A year ago I did not have a clue as to what I was taking on, regarding caring for her. At the time I thought I could do it on my own and I was doing it for the love of mum. As I have mentioned at the time I began to take care of my mum, I had no idea she was suffering from both vascular dementia and Alzheimer's. Yes of course I soon realised her mind was rapidly deteriorating and on the other hand, I had no idea just how severe it was.

Everything soon came to a head when she broke her femur the previous February. As I have previously mentioned decisions had to be made regarding handing back my mums bungalow financially it made sense at the same time the family knew full well mum could not look after herself. I needed to obtain the various benefits I believed mum and I were entitled to and would help to care for her. I also made contact with various local care homes, to find out if they ran daycare centre's, so that I could have some time off from looking after my mum and to have a break from both the physical and the mental stress of providing full time care for mum. When I informed mum of what I was planning she was totally against it.

She reacted and whenever I broached the subject of vascular dementia and Alzheimer's which was destroying her mind. Also whenever those in authority (nurses including her GP) raised the subject she did not seem to react and just laughed it off.
Whenever it came to myself raising the subject she wasn't at all happy with me. But whenever others raised the subject of the disease she was compliant and never reacted.
There were many times when her mind would wander and she would tell me she had been talking to my late dad. At times she would suddenly wake up because she thought my dad was still "boozing" it up at a pub. She has becoming very restless and during the night she would walk around the house and would make lots of noise. I had to catch up on my sleep during the day, whenever possible.

I would like to reflect on what I perceive regarding mums medical care. I quickly became aware the NHS system is virtually on its knees. I felt mum was no longer a priority case. As she became at the time she was not a burden on the state. Only because she was living with me and I was caring for her she was not taking up a hospital bed. The four NHS agencies, District Nurses, GP surgery, the dementia teams, including the local hospitals and in my opinion they did not seem to be communicating with one another I believe it was because some of the agencies seemed to be on different computer systems. It is obvious to me if it wasn't for my having to coordinate with various agencies, things could have been much worse. I believe the hospital computer systems were on different networks. The surgery and the district nurses were on their databases. I believe by now the computer networks could possibly be integrated.

As time went by the district nurses were concerned regarding the fluid buildup in her legs. The symptoms seemed to be similar to when she had undergone a triple bypass years earlier. All due to a rheumatic heart condition along with leaking valves. I was wondering if there was yet another issue with her heart. As I write this story, I keep having to refer to making contact with her surgery, the reason I was informing her GP, regarding her condition was twofold, I felt I had a responsibility to mum and wanted to ensure she and I weren't "left to things" and secondary if anything happened to my mum and hadn't raised my concerns with her GP and if something happened to her, I would not be able to live with myself. In the latter stages of her life I was reporting the fact her health was spiralling downhill, that is putting things in laymen's terms. I was fully aware since my mum had been diagnosed with vascular dementia and Alzheimer's her health would over time deteriorate. At the same time when someone is looking after a loved one struggling with the disease along with a loved one not recognising who you are, it is soul-destroying and it is so hard to witness.

One thing about looking after someone who has Vascular Dementia and Alzheimer's it is the loss of balance and due to the damage to the brain and of course, at the same time the balance part of the brain is slowly being destroyed, as such a loved one will keep falling over. My stomach always did somersaults whenever I found Mum on the ground hence why many years before she lived with me, she was found on the ground in her village. It was the onset of the dementia and at the time I was solely concentrating on getting her eyesight corrected due to her cataracts. As the year 2023 progressed Mum's health was sliding downhill and there did not seem to be anything which could be done to alleviate her symptoms. The year would be the last year I would be caring for her and at the time the penny had dropped I knew it would not be very long before we lost mum to the horrific disease.

I have written the following chapters as a timeline of my mum's last months, I haven't gone into the "gory" bits as I think anyone reading the book will understand what was happening during my mum's battle with dementia. I want to describe what my mum went through and how quickly towards the end Vascular Dementia and Alzheimer's destroy a person. I have covered some of what was happening to mum in the previous chapters. The problem is when someone is caring for a loved one suffering from the effects of a horrific disease such as dementia or Alzheimer's, things seem to repeat themselves such as falls and pneumonia. At times someone who is suffering it will at times seem as though their health has improved and it then comes back with a vengeance. The following chapters will seem as though I am repeating myself. During mum's last month or two the falls had by now become more frequent and the falls were causing yet more damage. The pneumonia became more frequent the antibiotics were by now struggling to clear the pneumonia within her lungs. In mum's case, her vital organs were slowly shutting down. I also believe the consultants within the hospital and possibly mum's GP knew she was coming to the end of her life and was possible they did not know when she would eventually pass away. It is not a criticism of anyone who at the time were helping mum but if someone could have been a little more open with me, I think at the time it may have helped me to face up to the inevitable, this is only my humble opinion. I have previously covered when a stand in doctor spoke to me about palliative care and end of life treatment. I believe before she visited the house mum's GP may have discussed with the doctor about end-of-life care along with palliative care.

Writing about my mum's health journey is not straightforward, the timeline cannot be written in chronological order only because I found her health was up and down, one minute her health would be out of control and another time her health would seemingly have plateaued. Mid 2023 Mum was frequently falling over and of course the falls were damaging her body and luckily she wasn't breaking any more bones, at the same time, she had serious bruising. On this particular occasion, I was upstairs catching up on some sleep and after one of the nights where I was kept awake only because my mum kept waking up all due to her incontinence, of course I needed to see to her needs. Getting back to my mother's fall. I took one look at Mum lying on the floor and I could see both ankles were badly swollen and were badly bruised. I decided to call for an ambulance. The paramedics checked my mum and made the decision she hadn't broken her ankles. They then moved her into the house where they then carried out various tests they informed me her blood sugars were very low.

During one of her recent stays in the Hospital, she underwent numerous tests, and an ECG and the result showed that mum had an irregular heartbeat, which I believed had been previously discovered. One of the doctors believed mum had yet another infection and this time it was not a UTI. As such she needed stronger antibiotics; the antibiotics weren't issued at the hospital. The Doctor was examining my mother's stomach she diagnosed she had an infection within her belly, while the doctor examined Mum's belly she went silent and did not say anything to me, I could tell she was somewhat concerned about her stomach, she then used a handheld ultrasound on mums stomach, as I mentioned nothing was said. Nothing further was said and so I did not know what was found?

One other thing regarding Mum's health journey, she could no longer feel pain, which was somewhat of a dangerous thing, more so whenever she fell over. On discharge from the hospital, it was suggested I contact mum's surgery and to ascertain if there was anything my mum could take to help her sleep through the night.
I had previously mentioned this to her GP and on many occasions, we had discussed if there was any medication to help mum sleep, but alas due to her condition, she wasn't going to get any better and the Dementia & Alzheimer's the condition would only get worse, as the diseases destroyed her brain. He would not prescribe any form of sleep medication. Summer 2023 and once again I was becoming increasingly worried about my mum's health. Previously I had many conversations with my brothers including her Doctor regarding the inevitable outcome of her condition I could not see what was going on within her brain, by now it was very obvious it was rapidly being destroyed.

Often told me she had something to eat, I knew full well she hadn't eaten and so by now I was having to coax her to have something to eat. She was by now complaining of being "slightly" unwell and for my mum to tell me she was "slightly" unwell meant she was in fact very unwell. After my conversations with various medical staff and having read the information regarding Dementia I believed my mum was heading for end of life, as I was not trained in this area of health, so I was at a loss, deep down I knew she hadn't long left. At the time I was very concerned about Mum's condition as she was unable to walk properly, I had to help her to the bathroom and back to her bed. I needed someone within the medical profession to provide me with some guidance on mums state of health and allow me to prepare members of the family so we could prepare for the worst case scenario.

My brother Michael and his family visited mum and they had flown in from Dubai the day was perfect, the sun was shining. Mum felt a little unwell and as such she did not sunbathe as she normally would. The following morning she could not remember much about the visit, what she did remember a little boy, my brothers son, Alexander. My brother Garry often visited mum and his wife Faye and towards the end of mums life he also visited the house along with Michael. The summer months were much the same, by now she wasn't eating or drinking and she kept falling over. She was spending a lot more time sleeping and was feeling totally exhausted.

It was by now mid-November 2023 and once again I needed to contact Mum's surgery only because by now her symptoms were becoming so much worse. Her Doctor was away from the surgery I to explained why I was contacting the surgery. It may seem as though all I was doing was waiting until mum was getting much worse, but it wasn't at all, and the symptoms were by now happening over a day or two, as mentioned previously I am not a trained nurse or doctor, the only thing I was medically trained to do was basic first aid. Towards the end of her life, her condition became much worse.

Mum's condition was becoming far more acute and by now she was suffering from a multitude of symptoms all at the same time:

such as her breathing and the rattling within her chest weren't the same as the noise emanating from her lungs. Her skin was more pale looking and her hands and feet were cold to the touch, added to this her hands had a blue/grey tinge to the skin. She was far weaker and was extremely drowsy along with everything else her face was gaunt looking and she looked skeletal. By now she required me to assist her with all of her everyday needs. The list was almost endless and by now she was disorientated and she had no sense of coordination, her speech was limited and would constantly forget what she was going to say to me. Mum's balance and coordination were non-existent on many occasions, she looked vacant and would stare into space. It was awful and it wasn't going to get any better. I know this might sound uncaring, I have to say you would not keep an animal in the condition mum was suffering. As someone who is approaching the end of life their medical situation becomes more acute as such watching a loved one become worse is not a pleasant thing to witness.

The following is part of a message I had sent at the time to my brothers.

"As you both know I have been looking after Mum for @3 years and my life had changed exponentially. My social life and my ability to be able, to drop everything for instance, to travel to the Isle of Wight or the New Forest can not happen anymore. Almost every day I am walking through a minefield of arguments from the moment I get up until I eventually go to bed. As you both know it is soul-destroying. We all know it is not mum's fault as it is because of her disease. I am not moaning I feel I feel I need to explain myself. I knew sometime last week there was something wrong with mum but did not know what it was. As mentioned I was asked if I wanted mum to be resuscitated if things took a turn for the worse sadly I chose not to resuscitate. Rightly or wrongly as my thinking was if she had taken a turn for the worse she could remain in a cabbage state. I did not taken the decision lightly, what I did does keep me awake at night".

The vascular dementia and Alzheimer's would not kill her, it would be one of three things or all three. They are a stroke, heart attack, or pneumonia. I am not a perfect person at the same time I just want both of you to know I just want our mum to be looked after and to feel loved, as we all know she did not have a good start in life. I know I go on about my mum it's only because she is such a hard person to have living within the same house as myself and yes by now I thought dad was a saint. I also know why he used to go for a pint or two. After agreeing to the Do Not Resuscitate, DNR, it was difficult to assimilate in my mind and I went to the pub for a few drinks, I think reality had finally set in regarding mum's health". I spoke to the surgery's Advanced Nurse Practitioner, it was agreed to prescribe mum with another cours of 500mg of Amoxicillin.

I think the reader will have formed a flavour of how a carer also suffers along with the person they are caring for. They become sucked into the situation and look on life with tunnel vision. Their life evolves around the person they are caring for, and there is no respite. They become trapped in four walls. Towards the end of mum's life, she had persevered with the Doxycycline course of antibiotics, I felt it was far more important for mum to complete the treatment and to hopefully clear the infection within her lungs and to help make things less painful for her. I realised her GP or one of his colleagues would need to visit mum to once again check her lungs. I wrote to her GP updating him regarding her current condition.

Trapped

The pneumonia had never fully cleared from her lungs more so from the left lung. As soon as the pneumonia cleared up, with the help of a course of antibiotics then it would come back and with such vengeance. Sundowning had by now crept forward, in the past it would happen during the evening, more recently it crept forward to @3 pm and seemed to ease at @6 am the following morning. The arguing was by now constant and was unrelenting.

What shocked me was she was by now simulating drinking a cup of tea or eating it was whenever she is in a trance like state.
December 2023 for mum was not going to be a joyous or happy time of year for her. By now she was looking extremely skeletal it is an apt way I would describe her, for me it was a true reflection of how she was looking. By now she could no longer walk to the bathroom or change herself, or wash without my assistance. It was very sad for me to witness my beloved mum's decline. I was determined to have, if possible, one last Christmas with my lovely mum. My son and my granddaughter always had Christmas dinner with me, apart from the COVID-19 pandemic and the various lockdowns. By now and due to her rapid decline in her health, I decided to order the Christmas food online it had meant at least the food was ordered and all I had to do was wait for the day it would be delivered. To be honest, at this time Christmas was the last thing on my mind. Because of Mum's decline in her health at the same time I was ordering her Christmas presents online and on receipt I would wrap up her presents. Because of her rough childhood and she had a horrendous upbringing as such I always tried my hardest to make Christmas very special for her, I made Christmas her time, it was time to spoil her something rotten. My son Paul and Granddaughter Caitlin always made her Christmas a family affair and mum loved it. As she became much weaker I ensured all of her Christmas presents

were under the tree as usual, she tried her very best to guess what the presents were and could not believe the presents were hers. This particular Christmas she asked me what I would like for Christmas I replied it was OK she was adamant, so I ordered myself a 2024 diary. I do not know what I am going to do in the future Christmas's alas without her. As I write the book it is emotional, to think she will never see another Christmas. I and the family will miss her so much.

As my mum's health deteriorated I would tell her I would always be there for her and would do my very best to ensure she was well looked after, and she would never be on her own no matter what. I look back on the time looking after mum and my thoughts go back to when my dad told me to "look after your mum". I took on board what he had said to me, it was almost 62 years ago. Of course I stuck to my promise to dad. I do not know if he ever thought I would stick to the promise I had made to him so long ago, hopefully, I have stuck to my promise right up until the day of her funeral. I think back to when dad was seriously ill in Swindon hospital at the time his life was slipping away and he reminded me of the promise I made to him, to look after mum. So during my time caring for mum, and to be honest, I never truly knew how much dad had to put up with, living with mum, who to be honest was a bit of a loose cannon. It was obvious they were in love with one another.

Chapter 8 – Realisation

On Reflection long before my mum was diagnosed with Vascular Dementia and of course Alzheimer's. I and my brothers put mum's fall due to her poor eyesight and of course her cataracts in both eyes had they needed to be replaced. I thought after she had the operations her eyesight would have improved. Then she would be able to get her life back. To be able to return to her "normal" lifestyle and once again be able to live on her own to resume an independent life. As mentioned after having the cataract operations and then the COVID-19 pandemic got in the way. Alas her eyesight did improve but sadly she continued to fall over. To see a loved one fall over and to seriously hurt themselves is soul destroying and whenever they fall outside in public on their own it is heart rendering.

Whenever she stayed with me, I would spoil her with something rotten and at times it was like my mum was on holiday. The TV was commandeered by her, and she would relax at night watching her "soaps". During that time, she was able to go outside and walk around the garden and she loved "pottering" around, I have many stories and many memories of mum helping me in the garden. One memory stands out and it sums up mum, one day she wanted to help me in the rear garden, I asked her if she could weed the borders, bearing in mind the borders were in full bloom. I then carried on with the weeding in the front garden. After about an hour she came to see me and asked me if there was anything else she could do. I went into the back garden to look at her handy work, only to find every border was by now bare, there was not a flower to be seen. Yes, she had done a great job but there was not a flower to be seen. She blamed me for not telling her I had wanted her to leave the flowers alone. I managed to crack a smile, and we had a nice cup of tea and of course a slice of cake. What else could I say or do, she was right, I did not ask her to leave the flowers alone. Mum's life was never a dull moment as my brothers, and I were growing up life was always full of surprises. She was never a conventional mum.

This leads me to the initial stages of her dementia I wish to somehow peel away the veneer of her "normal" and everyday persona, away from the latter stages of her fight with dementia. She was a tough cookie and was used to looking after herself and as such she never asked for help from anyone even within the family. She was never the typical mother, grandmother, or great-grandmother and of course we all loved her to bits. Everyone knew what she had gone through during her younger life long before she had met dad. When mum and dad eventually met it was the best thing that had happened to her. dad on the other hand knew full well what he was taking on with our mum. One day in December 2023 just before Christmas I had to call 999 due to the serious deterioration in my mum's health. When the ambulance arrived, a paramedic observed there was an issue with her left lung. The paramedics then took her to the local hospital and A&E department.

During my mother's time in A&E, the doctor treating her had an x-ray taken of her chest and the x-ray confirmed there was a buildup of fluid within both lungs along with an unknown viral infection within the chest area.
Sadly, Mum's condition worsened and as such she was moved to the ICU Ward at the local Hospital. Where she then spent

Trapped

Christmas 2023 on a ward. On Sunday 24th and Monday 25th December, I was informed mum was seriously ill, and a consultant would not be examining her until Wednesday 27th December. I went to visit her on Christmas day sadly she did not recognise me. I brought with me some of her Christmas presents and she thought it was someone else's birthday, she had not a clue it was Christmas day.

I visited my mother on Tuesday 26th December, and my mum was by now seriously delirious and had not eaten much food over the past few days and once again she had lost even more weight.
I left the nursing staff with a copy of a Lasting Power of Attorney for Health and Welfare. At this juncture, mum was incapable of making any decisions regarding her care or her health.

Red Flags

One evening I went to visit Mum on the ICU ward only to be informed she had been moved to another ward.
I was a little taken aback, because during my previous visit to the ward mum's delirium was much worse, normally she would eventually recognise me but not on this visit, it was just as though I was a stranger. Normally it would mean there was an underlying issue.

When I reported my observations, I was informed mum was taking oral antibiotics due to a viral infection within her lungs.
During her stay on the ward, I was informed mum's legs, and her lungs were once again full of fluid and by now she was on an IV of antibiotics to help to clear the lungs at the same time to try to clear up an unknown viral infection.

Trapped

She would need to remain in the hospital until a consultant could authorise an echo scan to be able to view the results of the scan, afterwards, the team would then be able to formulate a plan for her medical care. I was so concerned regarding my mother's health due to the following reasons:

I visited Mum on the 26th of December, I found her in a delirious state, and she had not eaten much food the past few days and she lost yet more weight, her intake of fluid was low, and I found she had not been drinking any fluids. Once again, I left the nursing staff a hard copy of the Lasting Power of Attorney for Health and Welfare. At this juncture my mum was incapable of making any decisions regarding her care and of course her health. During a conversation with a nurse in a previous Ward I was informed mum might be able to go home and to come back to the hospital as an outpatient for an echo scan. This raised a "red" flag, such as what has changed since my mother was admitted to A&E and having an x-ray taken showing a lot of fluid within her lungs and legs. To go to another ward and without having another x-ray to help show the fluid had stopped leaking from her heart. I believe my mother had been moved to dare I say it, to free up a bed. My concerns were at the time and were many and if she came home the cycle of her lungs filling up with fluid, would happen again and again I would then have to phone 999 to have her admitted to A&E, and so once again the cycle would then start all over again and by now her health was becoming a vicious circle. In and out of hospital.

Under the authority of the Legal Power of Attorney for Health and Welfare and due to my mum's ongoing ill health due to Vascular Dementia and Alzheimer's, I had the authority to enable Mum to have "life-sustaining medical treatment".

Trapped

My mother was back home with me, and she had by now been discharged from the hospital I must point out my mother's mental health was far worse than when she entered the hospital. She was crying all the time and could not seem to settle at night. She did not have a clue as to where she was. For me It was a huge shock to see her deterioration. Even though I had tried to nurse her through the rapid deterioration in her health I do not think she should have been discharged. To me it was as though the hospital had virtually "dumped" her on me, and it was now up to me to sort out the repercussions.

By early January 2024, she was discharged from the hospital, and she had ongoing medical issues. During her last visit to the hospital, a consultant on the ward confirmed the following:
A CT scan of her brain found she had sadly suffered from multiple "mini strokes". An echo scan showed an enlarged heart and was by now shaped like a balloon and a heart valve was damaged. Hence, I believe was the cause of the build-up of fluid within her body. She had a dilated proximal ascending aorta – The dilated or aneurysmal ascending aorta was at risk of a spontaneous rupture or dissection. – which means there is a high case of it rupturing at some time. I was also informed due to the build-up of fluid my mum's kidneys were by now diseased. I read my mother's discharge document because I was given a copy, and I could see that mum had chronic kidney disease N18 – which means end-stage renal disease. This was obviously serious and on discharge, it had been noted her renal function was not returned to a healthy baseline mum was assessed as being at a substantial risk of blood clots – Once again something I am not trained to spot or even be aware of.

Trapped

During the last days, Mum stayed with me after her discharge from the hospital, I observed over three days my mum was "off" her food and had no appetite. She was "off" her food in the hospital as such she had lost a vast amount of weight, and she was gaunt looking. My mum continued to lose weight. I once again raised the point mum was no longer eating and had lost her appetite. She had once again been placed on 40mg of furosemide, over the past three days and only passed urine three times a day. This is not her normal frequency of passing urine. Her legs and feet were very cold to the touch, so far there does not seem to be any swelling, not yet anyway. I did have some issues regarding her recent discharge from the hospital. She was in such poor health to me; it seemed as though she was sent home only because there was an urgent need for beds on the ward. I was her carer and living within the Winchester district as such my mum was deemed "healthy" enough to be discharged to my home. I was her carer; it was difficult enough to carry out the everyday chores such as trying to keep her clean and fed. Since leaving the hospital she no longer slept throughout the night, and she was waking up crying and shouting because she did not know where she thought she was still in hospital. I believe having recently been admitted to the hospital had a profound effect on mum's health.

I kept telling various NHS agencies I was not a trained medical expert, I must have sounded at the time like a parrot, having to repeat myself, I believe mum was discharged from the hospital in an unfit state, health wise, and as such she was not at all well and I had no compulsion but to call 999 once again to repeat the process, over and over again. I am afraid I had lost my confidence in the NHS System as a whole. I had many red flags and alarm bells ringing, and all regarding my mum's care under the NHS. At

this point, and because of her declining health it was at this point someone from the surgery or within the NHS "system" needed to speak to me and the family regarding "End of Life Care" or Palliative Care". The meaning of end-of-life care is for someone who has an advanced Incurable Illness, such as dementia and is frail, and she also had co-existing conditions, i.e. Heart and Valve issues along with kidney disease along with mini-strokes.
If the consultants at the Hospital were telling me, they could no longer operate on mum's heart. It seemed to be her heart that was the underlying issue and of course she had many other issues, and it would suggest the oedema and AKI could be managed but could not be cured which in turn did not paint a very good picture for mum's future.

It also implied mum's heart was a problem and was not producing enough blood, this either caused or was separate from edema and pulmonary edema (legs and lungs) which in turn had led/linked to AKI. On the 1st of January 2024, my mum had once again been admitted to the local hospital, on the authority of the "Virtual Ward" team. My mother's health continued to decline and I did believe her overall health was being overlooked, I say this because when she was admitted to the hospital the doctors were only looking at a specific issue and not at her overall health and as such were missing the core issues. During the following morning, I contacted my brothers as I was waking up early because I could not sleep, mum was by now on my mind all the time.

I could not settle; my mind was going ten to the dozen. I felt guilty for having placed Mum in the care of the staff at the hospital, I know I may come across as an angry son, I am not and it could not be further from the truth but I was becoming somewhat frustrated only because I had to repeat mums medical history each time she was admitted to hospital and her overall health was not targeted as such things were being missed. I am now having to fight for mum's care, I forgot to mention I needed to point out she had lost her appetite and had not eaten a full meal since she was initially admitted to the hospital, it was by now early January 2024. On one of the wards, she was looking skeletal when I visited her, I had witnessed her refusing her lunch. At the time I was not sure if it was linked to other medical issues. As previously mentioned, the doctors did not seem to be looking at my mum's overall health, they seemed to only be looking at her fluid issue not her vascular dementia. A junior doctor recorded our concerns, I also wrote to mum's GP and once again laying out my concerns regarding mum's health. I have laid out in the following paragraphs the timeline of events when my mum was admitted to the hospital. I realised a letter was not going to get anything resolved but hopefully, another 89-year-old lady or gent does not have the same experience as my mum. At the time I knew members of the medical teams would have to stick together.

I do realise every A&E department are fully stretched my experience concerning my mum they seemed to have lost their core values and the moral compass. I do not think they were geared up to help someone who is suffering with a mental health issue, such as dementia. Respect, Dignity, Compassion, Improving Lives, working together for patients, On Monday the 1st of January 2024 I was contacted by a nurse who called me from the "virtual ward" at our local hospital, who introduced herself. She informed me she was calling to check to see if I had any contact with the district nurses, regarding the taking of blood from mum. As mentioned, the previous Friday the 29th of December 2023

Trapped

she was discharged from the hospital ward, and I was informed a district nurse would contact me to take blood from my mum. The blood results were to be uploaded to the virtual ward team. I confirmed the district nurses' team was in contact with me and she gave me a date for when she was going to visit the house. It was at this point the Nurse from the virtual ward asked me how my mum was feeling after having recently been discharged from the hospital. I informed her mum had been hallucinating during the night of Saturday night (30th December 2023) and it looked once again like mum's legs had filled up with fluid, I pointed out I did not like the look of her left leg because it was a dark colour. Earlier the same morning she was complaining of feeling dizzy also her balance was a huge issue for her. She could not walk to the bathroom, and I had to move a kitchen chair for her to rest on. Then between us, we managed to get her into the bathroom.

After more questions, the nurse informed me, she felt she now needed to speak to a doctor regarding my mother's symptoms and to see if they had warranted her being once again being admitted to the hospital, it was at this point I asked if someone could visit my home and she replied she would check and would get back to me.

10-20 minutes later the same nurse phoned me back and informed me she had indeed spoken to a doctor they were concerned regarding my mother's health and to be 100% sure they needed to see my mum in hospital. The nurse went on to inform me she had already arranged an ambulance to bring mum to the A&E department the nurse would also inform the A&E department of my mother's arrival, and she would request a bed on a ward.Soon after the call from the virtual ward team, the South-Central Ambulance Service 999 control centre informed me they had received an urgent request from the hospital to convey mum to A&E, approximately two hours later an ambulance with paramedics arrived at the house. After examining my mother, they informed me there was a backlog of ambulances outside of the A&E department and it would be 3-4 hours to offload patients into A&E. The paramedics informed me it would be far quicker to take my mother to A&E by car. I went on to explain to them my mum was very frail and she was suffering from vascular dementia and Alzheimer's and had been recently discharged from a ward at the hospital having suffered at some stage of mini-strokes within her brain, also an issue with her heart and diseased kidneys, the paramedics helped to get my mum into my car.

At the hospital's A&E department, I had to ask two paramedics to assist me to get my mum from out of the car. The paramedics assisted in getting her inside the A&E department and into the reception area. Whereupon I "booked" mum into A&E. At one stage I had to leave mum on her own, to move my car from outside of the ambulance bay area. When I returned it was approximately 15:30. We then waited a nurse took mum to a cubicle to book my mum into the A&E system and to arrange bloods, at this stage there seemed to be a problem, I was once again informed the nurse who had phoned for an ambulance to bring my mum into A&E and it was arranged by someone from the virtual ward team. Still, the nurse had an issue, I rang the virtual ward and got through to a different nurse. She informed me the ward had not contacted me and had not arranged for an ambulance to bring mum into the hospital, by this time the nurse booking mum into A&E and found some notes regarding my mother's arrangements to access care at the hospital.

Trapped

She informed me it was not the correct procedure; mum would have to process her into A&E. It was at this point the nurse who I spoke to earlier, whilst at A&E, phoned me and she informed I would have to find a doctor or a consultant to arrange for my mum's admittance as the people who worked on the virtual ward would not have authorised my mum coming into the hospital as there were no beds free for her, I informed her it was not my job to "run around" and arrange for mum to be admitted. I told her it was not the way for me to arrange things within the hospital the call suddenly ended, the person I was talking to cut me off.

By this time, the A&E nurse spoke to her duty doctor and the nurse took me to a room for Mum to have her bloods taken and for her blood pressure to be read along with her temperature. The A&E nurse informed me there were no beds within the hospital, and I once again informed her it was a nurse on the virtual ward who had asked me to bring my mum to the hospital, as such I assumed a bed was waiting. Due to my mum's frailty, she was wheeled to the central A&E waiting room. By now it was @17:00. Bearing in mind my mother had only 48 hours before arriving at A&E and had previously been discharged from a ward. Having been subjected to various tests:
Such a CT scan where it was discovered mum had recently suffered from mini strokes. Along with an x-ray and an echo sound it had also been discovered her heart had become enlarged and it was shaped like a balloon and a valve within her heart had thinned and it was the cause of the buildup of fluids. Along with everything else it was also found she had kidney disease due to the buildup of fluid within her body and of course, her kidneys had been submerged in fluid, which had by now diseased her kidneys.

Trapped

I was informed by a nurse, in A&E was busy, and we would have to wait a few hours to be seen. By now mum was becoming very thirsty and peckish, good job there was plenty of water available along with some biscuits. During the wait two different A&E nurses at various times of the evening addressed mum by her name they asked her to confirm her birthdate and took her blood pressure along with her temperature.

The hours passed by and after 8 hours of waiting, my mum was by now hallucinating and by this stage she was well into her sundown period and was extremely confused. I walked back to the waiting area, thinking surely someone would come to see and to check on mum, it was a difficult time because by now she was delirious and crying. I sat across from the doctors and nursing workstation area, I could not help but hear the same doctor speak to someone on the phone regarding mum and I could not help but hear what was being said.

I naturally assumed the doctor would come over and talk to me regarding mum, I could see she was busy so I gave her the benefit of the doubt, I patiently waited roughly for half an hour later, the doctor carried on working and did not come over to talk to me. I got up out of the chair and was once again stood just outside of the working area the same doctor was standing close by, I once again politely asked her if there was an update on my mum's condition, whereby she replied to the effect, "you can't just walk in off the street and expect to be seen", once again I calmly but firmly pointed out the sequence of events by this time I could hear mum crying behind me. I was shocked by the doctor's response, she shouted "go away you have stood there and have disrespected me", by now I had just about as much as I could take and I replied, "I have not disrespected you, I was only trying to

Trapped

explain how and why my mum has ended up here and to point out to you I have not just walked in off the street, as you put it". She said something about it being another department who should have seen your mum and had made a mistake. I said, "It is you who has disrespected my 89-year-old mother who is extremely unwell". I pointed out to her my mum had recently been discharged from one of the wards and had recently suffered from mini-strokes I pointed out I did know why she was unwell hence why a virtual ward, nurse had arranged for mum to come into the hospital for further investigations.

When I returned to my chair in the A&E area three people approached me and told me they heard everything and in fact it was the doctor who was disrespectful towards me and mum, they thought I was only trying to point out what was wrong with mum and would have done the same thing if they were in my shoes.
I got the feeling I should have known about A&E protocols ?? and how the department was being run. The doctor's patient care was non-existent, and it left a lot to be desired, perhaps some sort of refresher course on how to be more caring towards elderly patients was needed? But there again they are doctors trying to safe peoples lives on the front line.

After @10 hours a doctor from another ward, perhaps from an intensive care ward? examined mum and after examining her he then asked me several questions and one of them was along the lines of "why did you decide to bring your mother into A&E I once again reiterated about the story of a nurse from the virtual ward having arranged for my mum to come into hospital. We were once again told to take a seat in the A&E waiting area. It was by now approaching 12 hours after having arrived in A&E and mum still had not been moved onto a ward, I was oblivious to what

Trapped

decisions were being made regarding our situation. It was at this point I saw the same doctor who had earlier examined my mum a few hours previously. I asked him when it would be when mum was going to be admitted onto a ward, he replied he did not have any idea.

Fifteen hours later poor my mum was finally moved to a ward. It was now 4 am the following morning I left my mum in the capable hands of the ward staff. There were no doctors or consultants available at that time of the morning. On the 3rd of January 2024, Mum was discharged from the ward. The same afternoon I had a phone call from someone called Michael who is part of the hospital's dementia team, I had previously met him when Mum was on a ward over Christmas. He asked me if I had any concerns regarding mums vascular dementia and Alzheimer's, I told him I was very unhappy about the 15-hour wait in A&E and at the time mum was hallucinating and she was extremely delirious and was crying , because by now she was suffering with her sundowning syndrome, I was very concerned and had tried my hardest to explain, mums condition to an A&E doctor. I explained to Michael the challenging work to get a very frightened mother into a routine at home had by now been undone during the horrendous time at the hospital. It has gotten to the state whenever the word hospital was used, she would tell me she never wanted to go anywhere near a hospital ever again. It was nighttime on the 3rd of January 2024 she was crying in bed, she was at home and was weeping and told me "It was horrible in that hospital, please promise me you won't let me go in there again". I had to agree with her as I knew it had been a horrendous experience for her.

Trapped

By now Mum was not eating or drinking anything and she was staying in bed .and had lost her zest for life. This is quite common in the latter stages of dementia or the last stages of life. It is a vicious circle that develops as the person reduces their intake of food and fluids. This in turn causes the body to react by conserving energy as such the person becomes more immobile and is more likely to sleep all the time. Then there is a cycle of "no food or very little food versus sleep" scenario. You often find because someone is peaceful and sleeping and at the same time, they are not taking on board food or fluids you wake them to take fluids etc onboard or just let them sleep. This leads to a scenario where insufficient food and fluids are being consumed to be compatible with life, unfortunately. As someone moves towards the end of life the sleeping becomes longer and where the body previously tried to conserve energy, it now moves onto the stage of protecting the major organs and often there is not enough to go around. This can mean there is a build-up of toxins within the body, and this can cause people to sleep even longer still. Eventually, the organs begin to shut down. You will notice less urinary output for example, as the kidneys stop functioning. This continues until death occurs. As this was happening, someone urgently needed to assess mum at home, as she was still in bed, and she was very weak. I was trying my level best by giving her sips of fluids alas it was not near enough. She was at this stage complaining of severe back pain.

I spoke to the surgery, and it was suggested I should message them with my concerns, at the same time I also messaged my brothers.

Trapped

I have to say there was no way I was going to allow mum to go anywhere near the local A&E. Even though I knew at this point she was dying, and she did not have long left with the family.

If she was indeed in the last days of her life and she needed to be assessed formally by a dementia specialist via a house visit as the A&E system was not working. It was proved to be a very poor service from the NHS if I was right and to be honest, I knew better than anyone only because I was caring for my mum on a day-to-day basis I could see mum was dying right in front of my very eyes. I must be honest I felt at the time the medical services were not taking my concerns seriously I did not know how to escalate my concerns. I was not being oversensitive or melodramatic, I was not being listened to, and it was so frustrating, I felt as though I was going around in circles.

Towards the end-of-life stage, mum was completely drained, and she was extremely weak, by now she was looking just like a living skeleton. She was still unable to eat and had completely lost her appetite. During her week's stay at the hospital, I did point out to the nursing staff mum was not eating any of the food whilst she was on the ward. During her two-night recent stay in another ward I not only pointed out the fact mum still was not eating. I also spoke to the doctor who was looking after mum and pointed out her total loss of appetite, it was by now coming on for two weeks and she had not eaten any food. Also, her fluid intake was seriously reduced. One morning she woke at 6:30 am I had a conversation with mum whilst she was still in bed. She told me she felt terribly ill, and she just wanted to sleep. She also asked for the illness to go away and to let her die in peace. By now the very mention of the word "hospital" was having an adverse reaction on her. It was by now late morning and mum was continuously dropping off to sleep, normally at this time of the morning she would have been out of bed and asking for a nice cup of tea. I believed she was giving up the fight to live, we all know just how stubborn and a fighter she was, it was her character, but after recently having been discharged from the hospital she had seemingly had lost the fighting spirit, and in my eyes she had now given up the fight to live.

My personal feelings at the time my mum was extremely sick, be it physical or mental. I still had not had anyone within the medical profession provide me with information regarding how bad mum's mental state was, or what to expect from now on in. Even though she had recently been admitted into hospital for the second time in only a week. On the medical front, there were a few issues regarding mum's health. There was damage to her brain caused by the mini strokes. There was also the issue with her heart and the thinning valve along with her diseased kidneys. One morning, as I cared for her, she was complaining of severe back ache.

I have repeated this subject previously, but I need to reiterate it only because by this stage in my mum's battle it is apt to repeat. It is quite common in the late stages of dementia or the last stages of life. Sadly, a vicious circle develops. The person then reduces their intake of food and fluids. This then in turn causes the body to react by conserving energy and the knock-on effect is the person becomes immobile and is likely to sleep for lengthy periods. Then you have the "no/little food versus sleep" scenario. You often find too that because someone is peaceful and is sleeping, they do not want to wake them to take more fluids etc onboard. This leads to a scenario where insufficient food and fluids are being consumed to be compatible with life, unfortunately. As someone moves towards the end of life the sleeping gets longer and longer it is a symptom whereby the body previously tried to conserve energy, it moves to protect the major organs often there is not enough to go around. This can mean there is a build-up of toxins within the body and can cause people to sleep even longer. Eventually, the organs begin to shut down. It is noticeable less and less urinary output as the kidneys stop functioning. This would continue until death occurs.

Chapter 9 – Goodbye

That evening we managed a good night's sleep and mum slept until 5:30 am. Later the same day, we were expecting a visit from Andover by a member of the palliative care team. It was a visit by "Beccy" from The Countess of Brecknock Hospice Andover and the thing with mum was, as I have previously mentioned if anyone was going to visit the house, I would have to drip-feed the details of the visit to mum leading up until the day of a visit. Beccy was excellent at talking to mum I have to say they got on very well. Also at the same time, she informed me what the palliative care team did including the support they would provide me and mum, and as Beccy talked with mum, she was also observing her. The visit was an initial assessment and during our conversation the subject of where mum wanted to pass away was mentioned, I know it sounds blunt and to the point, but for me there was only one place I wanted mum to see out her last days at home with me. Notes were made and Beccy mentioned a care plan and as far as I was concerned no one had previously mentioned a care plan, and she pointed out I should have been given one, at the time she had a copy of mum's current care plan. I checked a bag mum had taken with her during her last visit to the hospital and there it was, a care plan and at the time I had no idea it was there, because during my visits to the hospital it was never pointed out to me. Beccy went through the plan with me and she amended her copy to reflect mum's latest wishes to stay with me until her last days. She left to return to Andover and at the same time she informed me she would update mum's GP. A couple of days later mum's delirium was becoming much worse.

Trapped

She was only eating pieces of cake and taking in very little liquid. Of course without her drinking anything there wasn't such a need to visit the bathroom.

For the next few days, mum's health had rapidly deteriorated and by now she was looking more and more like a "living" skeleton and I could see right in front of me, my dear mum was slipping away as I have previously mentioned she was a battler of course she was putting up such a strong fight. There was an added problem and it was her circulation I could see that both of her legs were full of fluid. By now her legs and feet were cold to the touch the skin had a tinge of blue. The district nurses were still taking blood at her GP's request. The blood results came back after a day or two one morning her doctor contacted me and informed me mum's bloods showed up some anomalies with her liver along with her kidneys and asked me if I could keep a close eye on her urine including any discoloration. Her hallucinations were becoming more frequent one morning she informed me she had been talking to a couple who she had met when she was first married. At the same time she told me my late father had visited her, he told her someone was stabbed in the back. She was becoming more and more confused and it was heart rending to see my mum in such a condition, I just wanted to take the pain away, but alas I couldn't.

One particular night she slept for @14 hours and without having to wake up to go to the bathroom. A District nurse prescribed some strong skin cream for mums legs, as her skin was drying out, it came in a huge pump action bottle, and did the skin the world of good.

Trapped

Over the following days, mum's health became so much worse and she still wasn't eating nor was she taking onboard fluids. One morning during the early hours, I was asleep in my bedroom and while I was in a deep sleep I slowly woke up because I could hear voices and I heard a noise coming from downstairs bearing in mind over the past few days mum was finding it very difficult to get herself out of bed without my assistance. I got dressed and came downstairs and I realised the TV was on the sound from the TV was very loud. I opened the living room door only to find mum sitting on the couch and she seemed to be in a deep trance-like state. I switched the TV off and then she began to talk total rubbish to me nothing she had said to me made any sense, poor mum it was so sad. A while ago in my mind, I had lost my mum also I knew at this moment in time she was a living shell and nothing like her former self. I then managed to walk her into the bathroom and to get her washed and changed ready for the day ahead and to wait and see what the day would bring. Throughout the day she ate and drank a lot more fluids than she had done previously. That same evening she wanted to go to bed early and she slept through the night, it enabled me to catch up on some much-needed sleep.

Over the next few days, she was talking to people who weren't there and was once again talking gibberish, it was such a sad sight and I became upset. As the days went by she was becoming extremely disorientated and extremely confused, of course, I was so concerned about her memory and its deterioration, of course and added to her memory issues her speech was becoming so much harder to understand. By this time she was also asking where my late dad was, she thought he was still alive in her imagination and she had been talking to him and at this point, I was unsure if she was getting me mixed up with dad and by now her mind was playing horrible tricks on her. It was almost the end of January and mum seemed to have gotten her appetite back and of course I was relieved but naively I thought that she might be perking up. As she was eating and taking onboard more fluids. She was also sleeping throughout the night by doing so it helped me to catch up on some much-needed sleep.

Once again things changed and early one morning I heard a lot of banging the noise seemed to be coming from downstairs, I checked the time it was almost 2 am, when I came downstairs I could see mum standing at the kitchen sink and was washing cups. I gently moved her into the living room and I checked to make sure she was dry I then plonked her onto the couch. I made her a cup of tea along with a slice of cake. We watched a film and after a while, I could see she was dropping off to sleep on the couch. After some time I finally got her to agree to go back to bed, she agreed only if I stayed downstairs and so it was I slept on the couch. We slept until around 7:30 am once again I walked with her into the bathroom and then washed and changed her and I walked with her into the living room. It was at this period her speech was extremely difficult to understand and so we kind of understood our basic sign language along with the nods.
It was at this point mum was getting out of bed on her own and would wander around the house. One time when I woke up and I went downstairs, I found mum on the couch and she was sitting in the dark, she had no idea how long she had been awake. I then asked her why she was sitting in the dark, she told me the other people who were living in the house had told her not to switch the lights on. I took her into the bathroom only to find she was soaked and between the pair of us, we got her washed and changed. I took her into the living room and sat her on a chair I checked the settee and of course, I found it soaked. I then

Trapped

stripped the couch I placed the covers into the washing machine then washed down the couch and dried the pieces in the tumble dryer. In the past mum would tell me if she was wet but just lately it wasn't the case. Mum was once again aggressive towards me. This day it was time for a visit by the district nurses they asked me how things had been of course I listed the changes that were happening to mum once again mum accused me of telling tales. The nurses knew better it was time to take more blood from mum and to take her blood pressure and again it was on the low side.

Later the same day "Beccy" from the palliative care team visited mum. She spoke to me in depth regarding the end of care facilities at Andover and of course at the hospice in Winchester. She broached the subject of mum dying at home it was mum who had said "I want to die at home" Beccy asked me if I could cope with caring for mum towards the end of life, I confirmed I was capable of caring for mum during her last days? "Beccy" was then going to arrange for the "just in time" medication, it was to help someone who is dying and to help them die without too much suffering or discomfort and to of course maintain their dignity. The palliative care sister then left and outside of the house, she told me she had seen lots of people in my mum's condition and she wished me luck, and told me to contact the Andover palliative care team at any time of the day. At the time I honestly thought it would be easy to look after my mum as she was dying but alas and what I did not figure out was just how difficult it would be to look after someone who was in the latter stages of life and it would far more difficult along with the logistics of caring for someone who did not have long left to live also it would not be fair on mum.

Trapped

Once again one morning I was woken up at @5 am by the noise coming from downstairs I quickly got myself dressed and I rushed downstairs to see what was wrong with mum and when I got downstairs she was sitting on the couch, I asked her if she was OK she explained to me she had an accident in bed. I stood her up and I helped her into the bathroom and I found the couch was soaking wet. She was worried about what she had done, I told her it was OK as everything could be washed. Inside the bathroom, I noticed she wasn't wearing her incontinence pants and it was obvious she had taken them off. I helped her get washed and dressed and into some nice bright clothes, I then walked her into the living room and sat her down in an armchair, I stripped the couch and placed the covers along with her wet nightclothes also the bedding from the bed and I switched the washing machine on. I quickly made mum a nice cup of tea along with a light breakfast of Ryvita along with a piece of toast. She was upset and very embarrassed at what had happened the last thing I ever wanted to do was to take her dignity away from her, there was nothing she did that could ever upset me in any way, I knew I was losing my mum and at times she wasn't the mum I knew. As time passed by she became more and more aggressive towards me, as I have said before she was never violent. The following day it was time for "Beccy" the palliative care sister from The Countess of Brecknock Hospice to once again to visit mum. She may have had a call or was contacted by mum's surgery because she wanted to check mum's breathing and also the sound of her chest. "Beccy," noticed the colour of mum's tongue, she had observed it was brown and a little furry, she suggested I give mum vitamin C immune support tablets to help clear up her tongue. "Beccy" spoke to me in depth regarding mum's last days and also what I had planned for my mum, of course, I thought I would be able to cope with mum at home and if she passed away at home then so be it. She wrote everything down and explained to me if I found I changed my mind to contact her. The Hospice would make the arrangements for mum to see out her last days at the hospice. She said her goodbyes to mum and left. All of the people who came to visit mum be it the nurses the doctors everyone showed such kindness towards mum of course they were worried about me caring for mum and ensuring my health wasn't suffering.

Over the next few days, mum's health was seriously deteriorating. She was constantly waking up during the night and by now a circle of cleaning, washing, and staying up all night to sit with mum. Then during the day she was sleeping. The washing machine and tumble dryer were continuously in operation. Beccy had contacted the surgery only because mum's doctor contacted me, informing me he had prescribed yet another course of antibiotics for the pneumonia. The fluid in her legs was becoming much worse and her legs and feet were still discoloured. Mum was becoming very confused at the same time, I did not know what she was trying to say, and at times she was screaming at me to "get those people out of the house", her hallucinations were becoming so much worse. She would put her hands out in front of her to try to touch something that wasn't there and she was talking as though someone was sitting next to her. During the same afternoon, she dropped off to sleep on the couch, all of a sudden she alarmed me by shouting and once again she was hallucinating and shouting "I love my sons and hey you get out of here", as she looked at me.

My mum's aggressiveness towards me including the arguments was by now grinding me down, the fighting felt like it was by now a constant occurrence and there was no let-up. Even though I

Trapped

realised it wasn't my mum's fault, Dementia is such a horrible disease. The same day she shouted at me "Has your mum been in touch with you"? I tried to explain to her she was my mum and had given birth to me along with my brothers Michael and Garry. Her reply was "I didn't know that, it's news to me" My poor mum I felt so helpless, for so many years I did everything to make mum comfortable but now I felt so helpless as the dementia engulfed my dear mum. By now whenever she dropped off to sleep she had conversations in her sleep. The hallucinations were becoming more frequent and of course and of course she still wasn't eating very much or taking onboard fluids.

By early February 2024, mums condition was deteriorating so much and on an early and cold winter morning I heard mum crying out and repeating the words "oh god help me please help me" I quickly shot out of bed and rushed downstairs to see what was happening and to comfort her, I walked into her room and she said "where have you been, you left me". I managed to calm her to reassure her and to try and explain I hadn't left her, she wanted a glass of water as her throat was bone dry. She seemed very frightened and did not know where she was. She went back to sleep and I slept on the couch, and she eventually woke up at 8 am and I entered her room she told me she was far too tired to get out of bed. I asked her if she could try to get out of bed, as I wanted to get her to the bathroom, to clean her, and change her clothes, it wasn't easy getting her out of bed and at the same time I quickly checked the bedding it was dry. As mum walked into the living room she was complaining of feeling very dizzy, I quickly sat her down on a chair inside the living room where she rested and when she was ok she then made yet another attempt to get to the bathroom and once again she refused to use the Zimmer frame, by the time she got to the bathroom she was so

Trapped

tired it was due to the effort she had put in just to get to the bathroom and between the pair of us she got washed and then dressed in her day clothes. It took a while to get to the couch where I made her comfortable and switched the heating on. She had some tea and sips of water but very little to eat. When she walked with my help into the living room she was short of breath and sweaty when we were inside the bathroom I had noticed her belly was swollen and once again I became very concerned. During the day she was drifting in and out of sleep and she did not eat or drink much for the remainder of the day. I noted everything and I then fed the information to her doctor at the surgery. That night she fought me for suggesting it was time for both of us to go to bed, I eventually tucked her into her bed at midnight.

The following morning I completely forgot about a district nurse who was due to visit the house to change mum's dressings on her legs. It was 09:30 am and mum was still in bed she was exhausted, the nurse asked mum if it was alright to turn back the quilt for her to take a look at the bruise at the bottom of her back, she hurt it during a recent fall. She also carried out observations and took mum's blood pressure and also listened to her chest, she was not at all happy with mum's condition, so much so, she then spoke to the triage team at mum's surgery, I don't know what was said. The nurse then took me into the living room and told me she was not at all happy with mum's condition and informed me that she wanted a doctor from her surgery to come to the house as soon as possible. I fully understood that my poor mum was in a serious condition. At the same time during the nurse's visit, I was also in contact with the palliative care team in Andover and explained about the district nurses' concerns and about how over the weekend my dear mum had been suffering. I told the team about the nurse who was in contact with mum's surgery and hopefully, a doctor would be arriving at the house very soon. It wasn't long before mum's doctor arrived at the house where he and the nurse spoke in the room where mum was still in bed. The doctor came into the living room and he informed me my mum's condition had seriously deteriorated he then asked me if I could still cope with caring for mum at home only because by now he believed mum was entering the end-of-life stage. After the previous weekend and how much care mum required and I knew it was far beyond my capabilities I informed him I honestly felt I was by now incapable of giving mum the specialist care that she needed. I explained to him I had already spoken to "Beccy" from the palliative care team in Andover. He contacted her and he explained to me there wasn't a bed available in Andover. But roughly 10 minutes later Becky contacted me on my phone and she asked to speak to mum's doctor, after a ten-minute call the doctor came off the phone and informed me there was a bed available at the Winchester Hospice. I thanked the District Nurse for everything she had done by contacting mum's surgery and by now she had to leave, Later I contacted her bosses and I asked them to thank Tracy and the rest of the District Nurses who had previously visited the house to care for mum. Her GP waited for an ambulance to arrive to take her to the hospice. I thanked him and as soon as the ambulance arrived to ferry mum to the Hospice, he returned to the surgery. This would be the last time my dear mum would ever leave my house. It was such a sad occasion, I traveled with her in the ambulance and I got the impression she knew by now she did not have very long left on this earth.

As I traveled in the ambulance with mum and because she had been admitted to the local hospital several times over the

Trapped

Christmas and the New Year I already had two bags packed ready with clean nightclothes and mum's toiletries and of course her slippers. So as she was placed into a wheelchair by the paramedics I grabbed the bags. I sat in the back of the ambulance with her and I held her cold hand. It did not take too long to travel to the Winchester Hospice and as the ambulance pulled up at the front of the hospice, there were members of staff waiting for her, and they were so welcoming as greeted mum into the hospice, I know it may seem strange to others but for me, the welcome and it was so reassuring. Mum could not say anything and I could see she was too weak and extremely confused. Mum was wheeled into room number one on the ground floor the windows faced the car park. The doctors and nurses introduced themselves to me and asked me several questions, they were already transferring mum's medical files from her GP and I was informed they were currently looking at her files from her recent admissions to the main hospital. I was then asked to wait in the family room whilst the medical staff checked mum over. I could not get a good mobile phone signal inside the family room, so left the building and stood in the car park and contacted my brothers Micheal and Garry and updated both of them as best I could, I did say our mum would not be leaving the Hospice, we all knew by now she was dying.

I felt so guilty when mum was admitted to the hospice, the guilt washed over me. As I felt I had failed to look after her.
It was by now getting late and the medical staff informed me they were going to perform a blood transfusion overnight. I was informed I could stay at the hospice and I could also sleep in the same room as my mum but I did not wish to sound callous, I explained I hadn't had much sleep over the weekend and I just needed a good night's sleep as I would be stronger for mum and

Trapped

would be back at 7 am because at the time mum would be wandering were I was. I gave the people manning the reception desk my contact details and I gave them a copy of the Living Power of Attorney, I mentioned to them the DNR, Do Not Resuscitate. One of the doctors had made a note and said there would be something on her medical records. I was then asked to sign a consent form for the staff to begin mum's blood transfusion. I pointed out I was only less than ten minutes away in the car.

That night at home I could not sleep and I missed my mum, it was very strange without her being there. Because her "bedroom" was next to the living room in the converted conservatory I could see her bed, I had to be strong as a wave of sadness coursed through my body. As I lay in bed what I found strange was the silence believe it or not it was keeping me awake. It may seem strange but I was thinking, perhaps the medical staff at the Hospice might be able to save mums life and she would be able to come home and be her normal self sadly I knew full well she was dying and at the same time I did not know how long we had left with mum. The following morning after mum's admission to the hospice I managed to get there at 07:10 am. I spoke to the staff on duty and I asked for an update, they informed me a consultant would speak to me later the same morning. Mum wasn't awake yet so I went into the families room to have a cup of coffee and think about the current situation I and my brothers found ourselves in. I know people would say "Well you knew what was coming" regarding mums health, but when the stark reality sinks in death is such an emotive feeling and a taboo subject, for me I lost my mum a while ago, what I am trying to say, is once dementia kills off a loved one's brain, the person I once knew was by now lost forever, but when they are facing death in the face, it is a very different matter I believe nothing prepares you for that day.

One of the nurses came to find me and explained to me mum had just woken up and she was calling out for me. I popped into the room where mum was awake and was calling out my name, the nurses and the care workers were about to clean her and someone asked me if I had brought with me any clean nightclothes I replied yes there should be two bags of clothes, she looked inside a wardrobe and right there was mums clean slippers and her clean nightclothes, it was fairly obvious mum was not able to get out of bed. After the nurses finished I came back into the room and brought mum some breakfast, not that she was going to eat it. I made her a cup of tea in a special cup, it helped mum to drink her cup of tea without spilling it over herself. She said to me "How much is this hotel room costing you"? it transpires she thought she was staying in a hotel.

That night at home it was weird to enter the house without my mum, I found it difficult to settle and some people might feel they would be able to relax to catch up on some sleep. For me, it was very unsettling not to have mum with me. The house was so quiet without her. Once again that night I could not sleep and I was wondered what the following day would bring. The following morning at @7 am I drove to the hospice the staff were so nice and kind a nurse informed me mum had a bit of a rough night and she had been changed she was wearing a nice blue nightdress with white fish on it, it was one of the nightdresses I had purchased when she was admitted to the hospital ward over the Christmas period. I walked into her room and her eyes lit up I kissed her on the cheek. I had a bag with me with fresh and clean nightdresses, also her favorite cakes along with the cream for her legs. I handed the cream to a nurse and she informed me it would come in handy because mum could no longer get out of bed and the skin on her legs was by now drying out. Later the same morning I was informed about mum's blood transfusion sadly hadn't made any improvement to her condition and sometime and very soon she would need another blood transfusion. As the nurse was checking on mum, I noticed she was hooked up to a drip, I enquired as to why she was on a drip, the nurse informed me my mum was being drip-fed painkillers.

Later that same morning a consultant "Andrew" sat me down in the family room along with two other doctors, he wanted to talk to me regarding my mum's current condition. He confirmed she had a serious infection within her left lung and she was also losing blood internally. He went on to tell me mum was on an IV Antibiotic drip and overnight she would have yet another blood transfusion, it would mean she would have had two blood transfusions. What surprised me was when he said "if mum stabilised the hospice team would decide if she would be able to come home and if she did come home there would have to be a care plan in place". If she did not stabilise it would mean the internal bleeding was far worse than first thought, and she would have to remain in the hospice. He asked me if I understood what he had said to me, I did and I just thought "my poor mum, once again she is suffering". I said I felt so guilty all because in my mind I was handing over mum's care in the hands of others, I felt I had failed her and as such I was full of guilt.

I once again visited mum at the hospice and arrived at 07:30 am to be told mum had another blood transfusion overnight. Later the same morning I was informed by a doctor the transfusion did not help to improve mums vital organs but it was only early days and the medical team would be continuously monitoring the situation. When I was sat in the same room with mum I noticed she was still on a drip, I popped out of the room and spoke to a nurse regarding the drip, I was informed earlier this morning it was agreed to put another antibiotic drip into mums hand to ensure mums lung was cleared of any further infections. Mum was still asleep so popped out to the hospice car park and I updated Michael and Garry on mum's current situation.

Later that morning mum woke up to be honest she looked very unwell, it was heart rendering to see her looking so unwell. As she woke she smiled and I gave her a kiss on her cheek. I informed the nurses mum was now awake they asked me to leave the room as they changed mum and also washed her, I went to the family room to have a strong coffee and to once again reflect on the current situation, regarding her health.

A doctor then popped into the family room to brief me on what was happening to mum, she began by telling me, about the effects of the two blood transfusions and also pointed out the transfusions had not worked and mum was by now getting worse. Later sometime in the same evening, they would be arranging for mum to have an x-ray of her lungs. I thanked her for the update and went back into the room where mum had by now been washed and changed and she was drinking a cup of tea and had something for breakfast, which she did not eat. She could not remember me coming to see her earlier that morning. Later the same morning she became extremely delirious she was hallucinating. I informed one of the nurses and she asked me to once again leave the room I went to sit down in the family room. After a while a doctor visited me and I knew things weren't getting any better for mum. The doctor informed me there was nothing else they could do for mum apart from making her comfortable I knew what he was telling me.

The following day I once again turned up at the hospice early and I should find out the results of mum's x-ray of her lungs. I was informed a Doctor would let me know of the results. Whilst I was sitting with mum she spoke about dying and wanted me to promise I would be at her side, mums skin colour was tinged with a yellow colour along with a tinge of grey. The team were trying everything to alleviate mum's digestive system, I thought at the time there would not be too much to digest as she hadn't eaten hardly anything for days. It was time for the doctor's round and I was asked to "pop" into the family room. I knew it wasn't going to be good news. A doctor delivered the devasting news that my dear mum was dying and there wasn't anything else they could do for her. Even though I knew she was dying it was still devasting to be told. It meant all of my fears were confirmed, I fought back the tears, but alas it wasn't easy to do and my emotions got the better of me. I thanked the doctor for being honest and open with me. I asked her how long my mum had left and she said it was not long now and it was time for me to make arrangements.

After the doctor and her team left the room I contacted my brothers and I informed them of what I had just been told. My brother Michael was still in Dubai and on hearing the news he said he would arrange a flight back to the UK I then spoke to my brother Garry understood what I had said and would be traveling to Winchester. I then spoke to my children Sara-Ann and Paul.

After making the calls I walked into mum's room where I was informed mum was in a lot of discomfort as her vital organs were by now shutting down. I could see my mum was suffering her body had taken such a battering, it was hard to watch mum in so much pain, as I sat watching her I wished there was something I could do. It was devastating to watch my dear mum dying in front of me. During the afternoon all mum did was sleep, which was not surprising, one of the doctors suggested I go home to rest and catch up on things and to make arrangements, she reassured me mum was in the right place and they would contact me if there were any further changes in mums health. I said my goodbyes to mum and I left the hospice, I was very upset and so emotional. As usual, I arrived at the hospice early just as the nurses were changing mum's bed I left a clean nightdress for mum to wear for the day. I left to sit inside the family room and reflected on the future without mum. The hospice was quiet and felt so peaceful not like the main hospital wards where mum stayed over Christmas.

My brother Garry was traveling from Bridlington to be with mum. One of the nurses asked me whenever I next visited the hospice could I bring with me some day clothes so they could dress mum when she eventually passed away for her to wear when she was taken from the hospice by the undertakers. It did shock me but at the same time, I fully understood the reason why these things had to be confronted and needed to be addressed. To be honest I was already thinking about what mum would wear when she eventually passed away. I sat in mum's room and to be honest she was totally out of it and did not recognise me anymore I was very emotional. I informed the reception team my brother Garry would be arriving at some stage the same day. As mum lay in the hospital bed, one of the nurses asked me if I wanted to go for something to eat and to get some quiet time, they would keep a close eye on mum and they would contact me if there were any changes. I went to the canteen on the hospital site where I then contacted my brother Michael he confirmed he had made arrangements to fly home. I had a bite to eat and read the papers I then walked back to the hospice where mum was half awake and was hallucinating and she was calling out. One of the doctors who was caring for mum briefed me regarding what the hospice could do for mum, we spoke in the family room, she pointed out, some elements regarding mum's health. I already knew, and was informed the blood transfusions hadn't improved her health and the antibiotics weren't working either I knew my mum's vital organs were slowly shutting down the only medication mum would be taking would be strong painkillers.

By now Garry arrived at the hospice and he was briefed by the clinical matron along with a doctor regarding mum's condition and also what was going to happen next. We spoke and we knew it was only a matter of time before mum passed away.
As we sat with mum it was fairly obvious to both of us she was by now totally exhausted and was drifting in and out of sleep, Garry kissed her and we decided to return to my house later on that evening, we went for a meal at the local pub. Whilst we were there we had a long conversation regarding mum's condition. We then walked back to my house where I tried my very best to get some sleep, I told Garry I would be visiting the hospice as usual somewhat early the next morning. Garry said he would follow later on as he had driven from Bridlington since 08:00 am and was exhausted. Before I left the house I placed the clothes along with the shoes I wanted mum to wear at her funeral. When I arrived at the hospice a nurse placed mum's clothes on a hanger inside a wardrobe inside her room. I was told mum had another rough night, I looked at mum and she was asleep and looked all in. I informed the hospice staff I had been in contact with a

Trapped

funeral directors I gave them the details. Once again as I sat with her so many emotions suddenly engulfed me and I had tears running down my face. I tried my very best not to show anyone how upset I was, but I am afraid it was a losing battle. Garry duly turned up and sat with mum and we chatted, we then moved to the family room and we spoke about mum I mentioned I had already made contact with a local funeral director. Garry informed me he was going to drive back to Bridlington the same morning and he would come back very soon. Garry left to make the long journey home to East Riding.

Once again I stayed with mum and she woke up for an hour or so but alas she kept drifting off, I knew it would not be long before my dear mum would succumb to the inevitable. I sat with mum for a few hours and she wasn't responding to anyone or anything. I decided to go home. At the same time I hated leaving her, but I needed to get some sleep to tidy the house and to wash her night clothes, to pack and clean her clothes for the following morning, I hated the thought of mum not being dressed in her nice clean nightdresses.

Later the same day I was at home and spinning around in my head were all of the things I needed to do, regarding mum. Suddenly and totally out of the blue, I received a wonderful telephone call, bearing in mind, I was very emotional and the ordinary everyday things did not matter to me, I was emotionally transfixed on my mum. The call was from what I deemed at the time an angel, it was such a reassuring call and it was "just what I needed" only because from out of the darkness a ray of sunshine shone through the darkness. I do think anyone showing me kindness during this particular period would have a profound effect on me. I was at rock bottom having "surrendered" my

Trapped

mum to the hospice and she was on her own, or at least that was how I was feeling at the time.

On this particular day 11 February 2024, it was my late dad's birthday. I managed to get to the hospice at the same time I had been arriving for many days. I was informed by the overnight shift mum had a "nice evening", I was also informed the nurses had moved mums bed to the nurse's station as she wanted some company they thought she wanted to be around people. I walked into the room where mum was waiting for me. We had a bit of a chat and then she drifted into a deep sleep and as she slept I could see she was gasping for breath. I mentioned this to the nurses and they told me it was all part of the process. I sat with her for a few hours and she was calling out in her sleep "please mother, please mother help me" and calling out my name. She was asking for god "help me help me god, please let me go" I was devasted to watch mum suffer so much, it had been a bad few years and this was to be the end result, I was once again emotional regarding the whole situation.

I could not take anymore and I had to leave the hospice, for me, it was ever so hard to see mum in so much distress and it was obvious she was nearing the end, it was as though she was pleading for it all to end. At this point, I did not think mum knew I was with her in the room. My mum was sadly dying and it was by now coming to the end of her suffering. It was time to plan my life and to look forward to a life sadly without mum. I had looked after her for almost three and half years and it was time to change my life and to come to terms with mum not being part of it anymore.

Trapped

The following day I made contact with the funeral directors they sent me copies of what they would provide for mum along with the costs. I once again visited mum and by now she had slept most of the day, at the time she was in and out of consciousness, poor mum, she was calling out and at one stage she called out "please take me, I am ready to go"

Before I was due to visit mum on one particular morning I had sent a message to the funeral directors I wanted to make sure everything was in place to collect mum when she eventually passed away, I know it may seem somewhat, cold and morbid, I have to say it is one of those practical things which has to be done along with a practical head and not an emotional one. The hospice had previously informed me they did not have a mortuary so it was best to make arrangements for the funeral directors to collect mum from the hospice. As always I visited mum and on this particular morning she was distressed and wanted to come home, obviously it was never going to happen as she was very ill and was dying. It was so heart-wrenching seeing and also hearing my mum who by now was in a lot of distress, at times she called out "where are you, granny"? and once again calling out "help me dear god help me oh god help me" and "Where are you Ron (my late dad), please help me".

I contacted my brothers to let them know the signs were indicative of our mum approaching death. One of the doctors and the Clinical Matron took me to the side where the clinical matron then informed me it was now time to call family members and to ask them to make the journey to the hospice. I once again contacted my brother Garry and he confirmed with me he was traveling from Bridlington to be with mum and he was going to stay with me. Michael had by now left Dubai and was in Kenya where he would travel onto Heathrow where his eldest son, Jamie, would be picking him up, from the airport they would travel directly from Heathrow to Littleton where they had already booked a room at the local pub.

Towards the end of mums life, I once again visited the hospice and on this particular morning she was awake before I entered the room the nurses informed me she had a rough night, I thanked them for the update when I entered her room, mum looked at me but she did not speak so I made both of us a cup of tea. I helped her sip some of the tea and she thanked me. I kissed her as I sat watching her, she was by now just skin and bones. As I sat in a chair she began to call out and once again she was delirious. I noticed she was back on a drip, I enquired with the nursing team about the drip and I was informed she had to be placed onto a painkiller drip. She was also given medicine to help her swallow, as swallowing at this stage was becoming very difficult for her to do. Garry was by now with me and he wanted to find out regarding the prognosis for mum, of course, we knew she was dying and did not have very long left. Garry was informed it was now the time for the family to visit mum and to say their goodbyes. He spoke to Michael on his mobile who was by now travelling from Kenya on his way to the UK.

I found it very difficult to see and hear mum in so much pain. I did not want her to suffer anymore, at least with the drugs which were by now being pumped into her she seemed less distressed. But I could not help but feel for her.
The following day I visited mum early as it was the routine she was used to, even though by now she was dying, there was still some flicker within her mind as to whenever I would visit her, I suppose it was when she woke and I would be there or on my

way to see her. Garry would visit later once again it was a very early start for him and he would have such a long distance from Bridlington to get to Winchester. Overnight I was told mum had slept for most of the night and was by now unresponsive towards me there was no response whenever I spoke to her. She was by now lying flat on her back I could tell she wasn't long for this world, my poor mum, I wish I could have her back with me.

Michael contacted Garry and informed him he had arrived at Heathrow and his son, my nephew Jamie picked him up at the airport. Garry took the call outside of mums room after the call, he told me Michael was coming straight to the hospice. He told Michael mum would not make it overnight? I stepped outside and I spoke to the funeral directors, I updated them on mum's current situation. I then spoke to the hospice reception team and gave them the funeral director's contact details. They had personally worked with them many times in the past and they would make contact on my behalf. As I entered mum's room she was somewhat alert but at the same time did not know what was happening around her. A couple of hours later Michael and Jamie turned up and I could see Michael was visibly shocked to see mum. A doctor asked if we could join him for a chat in the family room both Michael and Garry had many questions to ask, and because I had been visiting mum over the past twelve days I had already asked similar questions and I could see what the hospice team had been doing for my mum, caring for her and making her feel as comfortable as they possibly could. After the doctor spoke to all of us we then left the hospice to walk to a canteen within a local garden centre, and we had a conversation regarding mum and what was happening to her. Once we finished we visited mum's room, she was in a deep sleep. Michael and Jamie had booked themselves into the local pub and I went back home and

Trapped

Garry went into town to do some shopping. Later we all met up at the pub where we had a couple of drinks.

That night I woke up at midnight only because I had a very sharp pain in my left lung. I could not get back to sleep. Eventually, I dropped off and I woke again at 5 am and at 5: 30 am I could hear the landline phone ringing downstairs and rushed downstairs but alas I had missed the call. Soon afterward my mobile phone rang and I answered the call and it was one of the nurses from the hospice. I could not remember if she said my mum had sadly passed away. I ran upstairs and told Garry about the call, he said he would catch me up. I also told him I tried several times to contact Michael but he wasn't picking up, Garry said he would inform Michael. I got to the hospice within ten minutes and the nurse who I had spoken to on the phone had met me at the doors to the hospice and cuddled me and said she was so sorry to have passed on such sad news. I then walked into mum's room and it was obvious she had passed away. I held her hand and to my surprise, her hand was still warm, I then kissed her on the forehead and once again her skin was still warm. It was obvious she had only just passed away, but what I could not understand was by now it had been almost twenty minutes since the phone call. I was in tears and I thought to myself "mum at least you are finally at peace and free from the pain". I think she had hung on for me to arrive.

When my mum passed away Michael and Garry asked me if I was coming home with them, I said I would wait until the funeral directors collected mum when I looked at her face it was slightly contorted it was obvious she had struggled to take her last breaths of air. I wanted to remain with mum until she was taken from the hospice by the undertakers. I was still keeping to my

Trapped

promise to my dad all those years ago, to look after mum right up until the last minute. The undertakes soon arrived and gently lifted mum and placed her into a coffin on wheels and then wheeled her out of the hospice and into a hearse. I could not help but be upset, knowing it would be the last time I would be able to touch, to talk, and to laugh with her. Michael, Jamie and Garry went on to the local pub, in the village and to have a couple of drinks and book themselves into the pub for the night, of course our thoughts were with mum. I followed on later after the funeral directors had moved mums body from the hospice.

I joined Michael and Garry in the pub and as we stood in the pub my mobile phone rang it was the follow up team at Winchester Hospital, I was informed later the same day there was to be a meeting with the doctor who had certified mums death. The board would be going through the reasons for her death. If there wasn't anything untoward would notify the registrar's office of mum's death. I spoke to a very nice lady who confirmed there wasn't anything untoward regarding mum's death and would be informing the Winchester Registrar's office. She asked me if I was OK, because I had laughed, and she said it was a very unusual reaction, I went on to explain my mum was a bit of hand full and I had looked after my mum for twenty years ever since my dad's sad passing, it was now his turn to look after mum and he would be getting a right ear full in the heaven. The lady went on to explain what I needed to do to arrange the issue of mums death certificate.

That same night I had a decent night's sleep and woke at 3 am I turned over and I soon fell into another deep sleep and I woke again at 08:30 am, I hadn't had a decent night's sleep for years. The house felt so empty and I was by now trying to slow my brain

Trapped

down and not to over think things. I no longer had to think about my mum or have to plan or prepare things for when mum woke and have everything ready for her. It was strange having to only think about myself, I was finding it difficult to think for myself.

Before the weekend both Michael and Garry left to travel to their respective homes, as it would be a while before the confirmation of mum's funeral. With Garry leaving I was left on my own in an empty house and you could hear a pin drop. Each time I came downstairs I could see into the conservatory and the "bedroom" where mum had slept. The bed was still made and knew I had to dismantle the bed. That weekend my son Paul came to visit me, between the pair of us we took the double bed up to mum's "B&B" room where we reassembled the bed along with her wardrobe. I bagged up all of the bedding in mum's room and I placed it into the rubbish. By now the conservatory was empty I thoroughly cleaned it and scrubbed the floor tiles and washed everything with disinfectant, it was my mum's favorite cleaner. Along with bleach. It was the start of the first week without my dear mum, I tried to book an appointment with the local registrar's office without any luck. The house was so empty and at the same time, I was at a loss, for many years I was used to being so busy looking after mum. I then started to sort mum's things such as her favorite food and clothes, most of it was thrown out.

I was finding it very difficult to adjust to my new daily routine, because I had a very specific routine when mum was alive now I found myself at such a loss as to what to do. Things seemed very strange I was missing my mum. It was time to visit the funeral directors to make the arrangements for mum's funeral. At the time I hadn't visited Winchester city centre for roughly two years, it was strange traveling into the city and knowing I did not have to rush back to make sure mum was safe and sound. I was still thinking my mum would suddenly appear and her death was a dream.

Before mum had been admitted to the local hospice and subsequently sadly passed away, an NHS agency kindly submitted an application for various equipment which would have helped mum within the house. I received a phone call informing me the equipment would be arriving sometime the same week, I had to tell the person the equipment would no longer be needed, and they asked me why, when I told them the reason why. The line went silent and they said they were so sorry to have bothered me. It was the day to register mums death with the Winchester Registrar, I traveled into Winchester for an early morning appointment, it was an emotional time and it felt somewhat surreal. The registration went smoothly the registrar provided me with a code, that informs HMRC, DWP all of the pension agencies many of the government departments, and the local councils of mum's death the single code informs the agencies of her death.

At times it did not seem to have worked, the central registration of death that is, as such I ended up sending copies of mum's death certificate to some of the relevant agencies. A week later I was still feeling emotional regarding mum's death and looking back on things I suspect it was due to the fact mum had stayed with me on and off for several years and the memories ran deep, everywhere I looked within the house it reminded me of my mum. The funeral directors asked me to think about what kind of funeral and the service I wanted for mum. I sent photographs to my brothers and a rough design of mum's order of service. As I looked at the draft order of service I felt emotional as I knew she had left a huge hole in my life. God bless you, mum. I wasn't sleeping very well during the days after mums death.

Both Michael and Garry got back to me and had approved the order of service and they also selected the photographs to be shown on a screen during mums funeral service. I visited a florists to order the flowers to go on top of the coffin. I had a call from the funeral directors they arranged for me to visit their chapel of rest to visit mum for the very last time. When I visited the chapel of rest mum looked so peaceful and finally at rest. She looked as though the pain she had suffered during the past few years had suddenly been erased from her face. I am glad I saw her for the last time and for some reason I felt at peace and I had a feeling mum was at peace and was ready to leave this world.
Once again my house felt cold and so empty, I was expecting mum to call out my name, but it was never going to happen. When does the pain of losing someone ever end? Since mums passing my brain began to slow down, whilst I was looking after mum did I have to second guess what she was saying and of course her many needs. Right now I only have to think about myself. I was beginning to leave the house a lot more and it was a slow process. The funeral directors confirmed with me the funeral order of service had by now been sent to the printers.

I visited the local pub to arrange the buffet for the wake after the funeral, I felt a little more relaxed because all of the arrangements for mums funeral had been completed. Michael and Garry's families were booked into the rooms at the local pub, so it made sense for the wake to take place in the pub. Once again the palliative care, sister, contacted me from the hospice in Andover. I found it very hard to be relaxed as we talked about how I felt post mum's death, she informed me there was a

Trapped

bereavement team at the hospice and if I ever wanted to contact the team. She asked me if I had started the book "Trapped" and when would it be published. She is a very caring person I do not know how anyone can work within a hospice environment, as she once told me she was able to go home after working a shift within the hospice, so very true.

It was by now coming up for a week or so since my mum had sadly passed away and I wanted to thank the Palliative care team and everyone who looked after her so well, at the Winchester Hospice. I sent them a card along with a bunch of flowers, it was the same florist where I had ordered the flowers for mum's funeral, someone at the florist recognised the Hospice they informed me the flowers would be hand-delivered personally by a member of the florist staff, as her grandfather had recently been admitted to the hospice as he was not very well. I also wanted to send flowers to the palliative care sister who came to visit mum at my house, to thank her for showing so much kindness towards my mum, I was very grateful for her when she coordinated mum's care at the Winchester Hospice. At the time I thought a bunch of flowers would be a fitting and kind gesture for all of Beccy's efforts. I just hoped she would not be offended, some people can take offence at the smallest of things.

It was the 10th of March 2024 Mother's day, the day was difficult for me, as the garden in front of the house was covered in daffodils and reminded me of mum, because every mother's day I would cut the daffodils and I would place them into a vase for her. On mother's day she would have several vases full of daffodils from out of the garden. Mum liked flowers, if anyone wanted to cheer her up a bunch of flowers would always do the trick.

Trapped

It was by now the 19th March 2024 and mums funeral service was at 11 am. It was to be held at the 19th Century Chesil House, Winchester, and mum's coffin was placed in such a way with a view looking out onto the tranquil gardens with a view of a tributary of the river Itchen. Mum had a very fitting send off, she was born into a life of poverty but she had left this world in opulent style within a wonderful setting. It was befitting of our mum and during the service I could not contain my emotions and the floodgates burst open everything I had contained for such a long time came flooding out, the dam had burst. My brothers Michael and Garry did her proud reminiscing about our mum. My daughter Sara-Ann had never seen me cry before mum's funeral. After the funeral, everyone headed for the pub in my village where we had a splendid buffet and we reminisced about mum, Grandmother, and Great Grandmother. A few drinks were had.

I wanted to end the story of my mum's journey with the following points and observations. Before mum had been diagnosed with vascular dementia and Alzheimer's. The family initially thought her falls were due to her eyesight. Once she had the two successful cataract operations she continued to lose her balance and fall over. During this period the world was hit with COVID-19 and the UK was placed into two lockdowns. Which had hindered any further investigations into why she kept falling over.

The word dementia would conjure up in mum's mind, the spectre of being mad. During the early stages of mum's journey, I may not have wanted to face the thought of mum having dementia. I also did not have a clue what it would entail to care for someone suffering from dementia. I have to say the love for someone is such a powerful reason for looking after a loved one.

Trapped

I must add a few lines regarding the people who work in hospitals. I do not want anyone who has read my book thinking I have a bone to pick, it is far from the truth. People who work within the medical profession do a fantastic job. I truly believe the NHS "system" is under immense pressure as such I believe hospitals are much like a factory and people who are admitted are at times moved from pillar to post. My thoughts during the various times mum was admitted to the hospital I gained the impression whenever someone is admitted to the hospital they are processed and the aim is to then discharge a patient as soon as possible. It does not always work out the way the system wants things to work. The bottleneck is when it comes to an elderly patient who is not so fortunate to have family to care for them. The adult and social care in this country is diabolical I believe the majority of politicians pay lip service to the issues surrounding adult and social care in this country.

There came the time towards the end of mums life when I could not provide the best care she needed and sadly I had to let her go and she was admitted to the Winchester Hospice. I was very emotional when she was admitted to live her final days in a strange place. I have to say Winchester Hospice provided a loving and caring place, I found it very peaceful and serene.

I would like to thank everyone working at the hospice from the lovely cleaner, the reception staff, the nurses and the care staff, of course, the doctors and consultants. Everyone was so caring and they looked after my mum in a manners he would receive at home with me.

Trapped

There is one thing I did not know and it is all Hospices across the country are not fully funded by the NHS or government. They rely on charitable donations to help top up the funding.

Printed in Great Britain
by Amazon